"Street War"
...It's a battle to Control Your Mind
...Its battle to determine your relevance
...It's battle of destructive disruptions
...your Greatest Enemy Is Ignorance

By

Ritchie Felix

Publish Africa,
highcapacityworks@gmail.com
+2347036837775, +2348039202454

Printed in the United States of America

First Printing, 2020

ISBN 13: 978-1541011458
ISBN 10: 1541011457

Table of Content:

LIFE IS A PIECE OF JUNGLE

Every animal is businessperson, and do not ask to get employed by another in the jungle. In the jungles, for you to survive – you must have your own factory. You either own your own factory like the termites or have some kind of strategic *skill-set* to hurt for your own prey.

The bees do not trade its honey to get the cow milk. The vultures do not stay in the same neighborhood with the *eagles*, and the *spiders* do not seek for job in the ants' factory. Lizards do not take part in Olympic sports event among crocodile in the jungle. For a lizard to be a crocodile, it must first see the BIG PICTURE of the predator. It's not a function of having same body anatomy; rather it's about being raw, tricky, smarter, fearless, tougher skin, and having the ability to survive both on land and inside the water. It's about having:

The edge,

The comparative advantage,

The swagger dexterity

The survival instincts
The intelligence,
The hunch,
The tricks, antics, gimmickry, etc.

In the time of crises in the jungle, it's not the best species that survives; rather the most adaptable species survives and thrives in the jungle

In a typical jungle, there is no market for anything. If a polar bear kills any prey, it's for the family and not for trading. You produce what you eat or eat what you can.

Cash has no relevance in the jungle. Skill is all it takes to survive.

"With each new day in Africa, a gazelle wakes up knowing he must outrun the fastest lion or perish. At the same time, a lion stirs and stretches, knowing he must outrun the fastest gazelle or starve to death. It is no difference for the human race. Whether you consider yourself a gazelle or a lion, you simply have to run faster than others to survive".

...Mohammed Bin Rashid Al Mattoon

Introduction

"Robots could be soon flipping burgers in your favourite fast-food joint, pulling pints in your local pub and emptying your bins. Welcome to the brave new world of the service robot, where machines work faster, harder and smarter than their human counterparts - and don't take smoke breaks.

As armies of increasingly sophisticated robots are unleashed in workplaces around the world, technologists like to trot out their well-worn joke: A robot walks into a bar, orders a drink and lays down some cash. The bartender says: "Hey, we don't serve robots."

And the robot says: "Oh, but someday you will." The joke sounded funny a few years ago, but not any more. Robots are having the last laugh as increasing automation means that they are set to displace or eliminate millions of traditional jobs....." .... says Simon Rowe

Government policies around the world at the moment are not encouraging job creation but, rather shrinking existing job opportunities amidst the whirlpool of expanding virtual possibilities. What a PARADOX! This has created revolutions in different disguise around the world and sooner enough will graduate to permanent bloodless street revolution. Any average human will require a precision of adaptable talents or skillset to thrive in this kind of terrible economy. What will keep any soul tomorrow will not be traceable to stability of economy rather stability of adaptivity of skillset. How long a celebrity will last on the stage of significance for instance will be determined by stability of skillset not that of the economy. The era of "core competence" is now a mantra of old school economic intelligentsia and "fluid core" is now the new mantra of the global economy.

The government and ministry of education around the world are yet to do a tangible work to overhaul the antiquated curriculum and address urgent issues begging for immediate attention. This has further compounded the heat in the employment market and politics around the globe. It appears that there is a kind of conspiracy to keep the poor poorer and hold to ransom clueless souls that want to confront the corporate tigers headlong with own inventions. This continue to spark off fire of disagreement and instability in different society as more young people pour out into the streets hopelessly searching for none existing jobs and continues to be greeted with same old storyline. The wave of dissatisfaction is building up terribly every seconds and this will soon graduate to visibly rebellion of a kind that is not common. How long can young people hold on without job? How long can young people depend on the social security to run their life and express themselves? How long will young people stay by the sideline and watch at old and cranky oldies run the politics of the day? How long will the politician deceive the people? These are the few questions that must be considered by any machinery of leadership in the now.

One of the greatest undoing of Africa region at the moment is that, the largest countries in the continent except South Africa are not leading revolution in the terms of job creation, stability of national polity, technological innovation and full maximization of the growing "**Youth-Bulge**". Another major setback of the region is the inability to fully engage the growing economic bulge of the Africans in diaspora. The African nationals in diaspora constitute a major economic breakthrough for the region if there be a viable platform, plan and system to harness these seeming potentials. Most Leaders in the region are still in the old testament of the world politics, and steering the future of Africa towards old political parade. It's a complete myopia in highly evolved economic world realities. The continent requires continues streams of new ideas and dynamism to stay in the competitive market of the future. And this is perhaps possible when young blood drive the African Leadership at the apex. People of Old Testament politicians cannot get Africa anywhere in the future. They can serve as knowledge advisors at best from the sideline and not from the field.

WHY I WROTE THIS BOOK

Young people need to steer the affairs of the day. The Future of Africa is in **young blood** with or without political experience.

This book is targeted to help readers build knowledge in place and arm every reader with the armour to overcome:

#. Unemployment, Under-employment and Low-income

#. War of Machines in the job market around the world

#. Wrong Government policies and insensitivity leading to poverty of the masses

#. Rat-Race and beat the corporate conspiracy to keep people in the rat-race, etc

Also, this book **"STREET WAR"** seeks to prepare the reader ahead of time for the reality that cannot be avoided on the African soil. Africa future projection by the World Bank and United Nation statistics promises to be the hub of workforce of the world in the near future with growing young people population. The World Economic Forum Projected this data:

"In the long term, three powerful positive trends are likely to sustain Africa's growth. First, the continent has a young population with a growing labour force – a highly valuable asset in an ageing world. In 2034, Africa is expected to

have the world's largest working-age population of 1.1 billion. In recent times, it has had some success in creating jobs – 21 million new stable (formal, wage-paying) jobs over the past five years, and 53 million over the past 15. Stable jobs grew at a rate of 3.8% between 2000 and 2015, 1% faster than growth in the labour force. This is still far from the job-creation trajectory Africa needs to fuel future growth, but it is progress.

Second, Africa is still urbanizing and much of the economic benefit lies ahead. Productivity in cities is three times as high as in rural areas and, over the next decade, an additional 187 million Africans will live in cities, according to the United Nations. This urban expansion is contributing to rapid growth in consumption by households and businesses. Household consumption grew at a 4.2% compound annual rate between 2010 and 2015 – faster than the continent's GDP growth rate – to reach $1.3 trillion in 2015. We project Africa's consumers will spend $2 trillion by 2025. But companies will need to gather detailed market intelligence on where the most promising consumer markets are. Just 75 cities accounted for 44% of total consumption in 2015. Nigerian consumers alone may account for up to 30% of Africa's consumption growth over the next decade. Other segments to target include households earning more than $20,000 per annum in South Africa and Morocco, two of Africa's most diversified economies with a large consumer base, or those earning $5,000 to $20,000 in some of the fast-growing economies of East and West Africa".

On the last note for now, if you find yourself in a society where people have **strong plans**, then crop up with **strategy** to stay ahead. And if the people soon add strategy to their plans, it is wise you make your own strategy even **SMARTER** to stay ahead. And soon you discover they are adding up SMARTER strategy to their kits, then, add **tactics.** If they dare to add up **tactics** to their kits, then, add up "**FLUIDITY**"…as make up….just go now and read this BOOK to catch up with necessary ground elements to beat the "C-Suite" and be on top of your game. The pages of this book are loaded with quality content to transform your mindset and put you on the pedestal for super-royalty cum excellence. Bravo!!

Chapter 1
"Shocking trends, traits & realities"

In many centuries ago, war is usually declared before the real battle is arrayed in a specific location called the battlefield. The warriors involved in this warfare are not usually taken by surprise by their adversaries. Every warrior in this default world order knew who the marksmen were, their level of preparation and agitation.

Every warrior can tell about the sophistication of the enemy weaponry, and tell from which direction the enemies will launch their attack. The only decider of such warfare used to be individual's skill in wielding the armour in the battlefield. Possessing, developing and sustaining right battle skill used to be a huge asset to any people, community and nation.

At present, the matrix of warfare has changed so much in its composition, location and execution. In the last century, that is the 20th century, warfare transitioned from being a locational affair to become a digital affair. And in the 21st century, we now fight every day, everywhere and with everything. The minds of men have become the real battlefield and the hands now the shop window to display the discretion of the mind.

Everything around us today is either a tool for good deed or some kind of arsenal to invoke wickedness at a split second. Our streets are filled up with the imports of man's imagination, perversion of the mind, and the very obsession to do evil.

EVERY SOCIETY IS PROGRAMED

Today, every society is programed after the thought pattern of the ruling force. The society thought pattern of the ruling force. The society is more or less a manifestation of the structured thinking of its leadership. The societies of the 21st century, is like some kind of mould that are pre-programed to favor the most powerful, the most influential and the super-rich. Those at the lower rung of the ladder of the economy are apparently at the mercy of the ruling force. Gone are the days, democratic system seeks to build genuine consensus from among the people this day, it rather seeks the consciousness of the leader or that of the cabals – controlling the state art from behind.

In Africa, the leaders of the region are still seeking the economic template that will actually unleash the economic potentials of the system. They combs from America to Europe, and from Europe to the Bahamas, and to Austria, and every attempt seems to make even poorer, and probably more vulnerable to economic slavery. African leadership is yet to procure the Midas touch that will cause revolutionary evolution of the African market. The continent is yet to stop shipping coca abroad and start manufacturing own brand of chocolate. The process that leads to production of chocolate generates huge lines of employment opportunities.

The recent quantum leap in unemployment is a good indicator to the degree of mental decay, ignorance and decay-rate of ideas that has been in operation in the region. It appears the African markets areglued to primary production of raw materials and quasi-produces. Even, the African educational system seems to be structured to supply much needed labour force to build the economies of the western nations. It is difficult to advance the realities of the region to compete effectively in the comity of advanced enemies in the now in almost every sector of human endeavor. The Asian tigers built their own economics upon their organic reality and available content in their domain. By this paradigm reality, the Asian market took off in the 21st century and continued to build capacity to stay highly competitive at the global scene.

African problem is not the African soil. It is not the lack of natural resources. It is not the absence of arable soil for agriculture as seen in Jordan. It is not over-population as seen in both China and India. Africa do not have major climatic crisis. The region is only plagued by corrupt, clueless and unpatriotic leadership. Most African leaders lack strength of personal character, dignity and right competence for leading the people.

Absence of strength of personal character in the ruling force has caused Africa much havoc and damage that could be possible imagined. Leadership is first a *Content* thing before it's transcending into *Management*. It is the strength of characters that a leader musters within him that he/she brings to bear on the corridors of leadership. If the strength of weakness of a leader supersedes his strength for good character, the office of leadership cannotperform miracle or magic overnight. The true content of any leader anywhere is what programs the actual content that will prevail over the society consciously or unconsciously. Most African leaders are yet to come to terms with this reality. Leadership is not about winning vote/election; nay, it is not about competence without the strength of good character, rather; issues from the web of deep within a man. This is not media image laundering. It is not some kind of professional appearance that individual can pick up and drop at will. It is far beyond that. Until people with a stronger integrity fiber begin to emerge into the public spaces, the future of Africa is hanging on a balance.

Good character is a *CONTENT* thing not some kind of MAKE – UP. Every sector of the national affair including the local market places draws life from the central platform of government. Thus, if the central government or the apex government is faulty in its paradigm reality, content constitution, then every other thing draws and build upon the existing content pattern. This makes corruption to be endemic in the African society. It is the import of the leadership composition, and not the people thing as may have been suggested by different school of thoughts.

"There an adage that says, if the head is bad, then, the tail must also be bad". It is the content of leadership that pre-conceives the actual content that will rule over the society.

But, it is important to note that, the leadership of any society is drawn from among the people. Therefore, the people either beget the leadership over them or pre-conceive the reality surround the wheels of leadership challenge. How burdened are those preparing to go into leadership block of the society? How passionate or obsessed is the African leadership machinery? A true leader must be so passionate to own the problems of the society as personal challenges to an empirical fault. This is the Golden Fleece that is missing in the African leadership. Someone need to become so restless, insanely obsessed to change the statusquo and build stronger system/institutions. As obsessed leader need just little competence with great character mix to impact positively on the society. In some advanced economics, most leaders prefer to invest in the community spaces, and in the people and think less about personal gains. Such is the very opposite in the African leadership reality equation. Most African leaders prefer to invest outside the national territory because most times, it is the people money stolen and future that is carted away, and lodge all their investments in foreign banks. That has been the order of events, and this makes it difficult for the continent to experience rapid advancement in all it sectors.

Once the desire to improve on the state of things; and people ceases to be the obsession of a leader; the true passion, to move the territory under his governance become deactivated. At this point all manners of good character expected of a leader become short-changed, and corruption or call, it misplacement of state priority become inevitable.

Good character is a CONTENT thing, and never a kind of professional appearance one can pick up and make up. The unrepentant passion of a leader to champion the course of development and advancement of his/her people is first felt in words of the leader before it is captured in pictures. Leadership must be founded upon strong personal commitment to serve with clarity of mission. It is not something for an individual who is obsessed with selfish aggrandizement.

A TRUE LEADER MUST BE PREPARED TO OWN THE CHALLENGES IN THE COMMUNITY SPACES AS PERSONAL THING

The mark of a true leader is not in the number of cars possession, houses owned in different cities, quantum of currencies stashed in different countries, and number of mistresses that goes with your entourage.

That is huge error for anyone to think; that to represent a picture of a leader. But, it's funny to watch adult with better exposure in western education, politics and social economy behave as if nothing is at stake while he/she sit upon the throne of leadership over his people. A typical African representation of a leader's image includes:

- Massive mansion
- Private jet
- Fleet of posh cars
- Bevy of professional mistresses
- Massive currencies stashed away in different countries of the world

- Militant/terrorist connections
- Army of corrupt loyalists
- Expensive clothing
- Ownership of massive investments abroad
- Etc.

Despite what is contained in the school curriculum about leadership and the sovereign national constitution, an African writing thesis about leadership risk the chance of hitting below belt and score capital "F" in a global competition. Just ask a child about the image of a leader or what makes a leader in African setting. To say it just as it is at the moment, so many African leaders are consciously committing development crimes and cover it up with barge of excuses. In the advanced economics, one of the greatest ambitions of most leaders is to improve on the state of things and the state of the people. It is not really possible to put some African leaders on same scale as their foreign counterparts. Even, when the people do not want a leader to stay in the office in some countries in Africa, he imposes himself on the people and actualizes re-elections into offices using his paid loyalties. What a shame!

Someone asked me this question often *"What's really wrong with African leaders?"* I strongly believe that a leader's CONTENT of leadership beclouds the reality of the entire society. The leader is the real celebrity in every political economy; whatever that featuresabnormally on the reality menu of a society is a true reflection of the quality of a leader's content. It is content that creates traits, trends and norms of the society. The leadership of any people is their role model either for good or for bad or even both.

THE CORRIDOR OF LEADERSHIP IS NOT SHOP WINDOW FOR AMASSING WEALTH

A leader's PULSE for development is a huge asset to any nationhood. True leaders have unrepentant passion to own a specific challenge of the society so many challenges. Western nations are blessed with leaders whose heart pulse for development, security of the commoners on the streets, health-care for the people and advancing the economy of the nation. Most African leaders are yet to emulate this standard in practical term. Some countries in the region may boast about this on the research papers, policy papers and project documents, yet, much have not lifted beyond the pages where they are domiciled.

It is in African that people perceived Leadership as a shop window for desperate amassingof wealth. Most millionaires and billionaires in Africa owe their wealth to the political portal of their countries. In Nigeria for instance, politics appears to be the cheapest gateway to amass wealth, thus, politics in this famous nation of Africa is the real hub to access the common wealth of the people. The leader can even become far richer that the entire economy and still show face before development donors to request for loans or grants to carry out major projects in the country.

Let tell the truth: Leadership is not a career, it's not a profession, it's not a vocation, and rather, it's a "CALLING"...a SACRED CALLING. Leadership is

SERVICE that must be process with strong emphasis on "DUE DELIGENCE" and "DUE PROCESS" within the gamutof strength of characters, competence and clarity of mission. It's a complete RAPE on the people intelligence to loot the national treasury while claiming to serve their interest. It's an anathema of some sort – a conscious crime against development. The veranda of leadership is not a portal for self-enrichment. It's an error in practice. Until, Africastop producing leaders with bias for personal enrichment, the region would gradually and surely dissolve into antiquity.

Any day African Leaders wakes up on the right side of consciousness – African will recover. The, the region will produce leadership that has strong desire to develop the state of things and the state of people. Building stronger institutions and vibrant systems in all sectors of the society would be the obsession of those in power, and that of every citizen at large. The pursuit for holistic development in every part of the society will be the top priority of everyone. Once the issue of development becomes the very concern of everybody including the commoners on the streets, the nations of Africa will advance strategically in all fields of endeavour with unimaginable splendour.

CHAPTER 2

THE EMERGING OLIGARCHY

The drums of war are not beating for nothing. Africa is the next battlefield for the world war III. The region has the highest number of ignorant people, deprived people, and largest number of unskilled persons. Unemployment rate is exploding beyond the bars of normally in exponential progression, and under-employment has scaled up to a new pitiable height. Over the next decade the nations of Africa will come face to face, with the challenge of overpopulation, and out of every five persons anywhere in the world, two will be Africans. It's an emerging reality that will inevitably shift the boundaries of reality of Afri-shock and create a lateral tremor on the landscape of African governance.

Over the next decade, Africa will produce more fragile and failed States as new corporate governance would begin to emerge on the economic landscape to challenge every government policy and legislation. This might be very difficult to stomach at the moment because the faces of the monsters arrogating for economic power cannot be easily perceived in the present "*Holier-than-thou*" white-washed economic barbecue. Most African government at present appears to be clueless about this emerging oligarchy building up gradually but sincerely would dictate the temperature of the continent in every sector sometime in the near future.

The region has not really done much in building stronger institutions and developing systems with stronger ethical fibre. Democratic values, norms and practices have not really been deepened in the machinery of governance and entrenched in the minds of the governed, the right atmosphere that will enable all to thrive comfortable and participate in governance is yet to be created. Rather, only few people of course, political demagogues and power sycophant's including power-sharers that participate effectively and benefits most in the present governments in many African political theatres.

Every day in Africa; less than 1 percent of the continent entire population gets richer than the total 99% of the poor people. The super-rich that constitute the less than 1 percent makes their money from a kind of "HOLY ROMANCE" with the ruling power of every State in Africa Common Wealth.

The super-rich have fingers, tentacles and noses in almost every sector of the society. In some school of thoughts, it's believe that some cabals in the ruling forces operates proxy colony of "WHITE-HOUSES" being paraded as mega business enterprises own by super fellows. While other school of thought believe that there be some kind of conspiracy hidden from the eyes of commoners among the ruling the force to entertain the governed with various news items on constant parade in different news media platforms, and the powers that be continue to share the treasure that belongs to all. The later, seems to be the timely pictureof things at the moment when you decide to take inventory and put things in right analysis.

Check out the companies that declares more profits at the end of the year in every African society despite the odds and economic realities that even made ordinary people poorer. Check out those whose meal tickets are scaled up despite what happened in the market place and the challenge that beclouded the general polity of the state. Surprise, you will not get the poor listed. Check out those who broke into new market, new projects and others who emerge into Stardom and significance....surprise; you see that, there be a kind of state sponsored collabo to enrich few selected at the expenses of the rest 99% of the poor. It's a huge paradox. *Africa is shooting self on the leg!*

WHAT HAPPEN WHEN MUCH WEALTH OF A NATION CONCENTRATES ON THE HANDS OF FEW INDIVIDUALS?

Before you plunge ahead to guess the answer to this puzzle, I want you to have the following in the mind:

- What is the true content of character and personality/cartel involved?
- What is the dominant view, philosophy and belief system of the personality/cartelinvolved?
- What is the prevailing sense of responsibility of the individual(s)/cartelinvolved?
- What is the sense of mission of the entity or entities linked to these individuals?

- What is the sense of urgency of the individual/cartel mission in relative to comparative development of the state?
- Etc.

It's not oversight to state categorically here, that; Africa have not grown values enough to harness the development and economic potentials of the "super-rich" syndrome. In as much as the facts stated so far, this thought-line or rather submission appears to be debatable, fleshy truth with empirical evidence cannot be swept under the carpet. It must also be stated here, that there be super-rich people with golden mind, full of value-creation and have the right sense of mission to help the region to attend to her development dreams and realities. This cannot be denied or hidden in one's imagination. The purpose of this essay is not to critique anyone per se, rather to point the torch light in the right direction advancing the African dream and future.

If Africa leadership fail to grow or impute value into her institutions and people; ..the system will end up producing monsters that will disrupt peace advancement and probably mismatch the African destiny. Strong and vibrant institutions with concrete ethical fibre will create military force that will secure the region in the place of militants seeking for the enrichment of few people. When the wealth of a nation is in the hands of right people, the economy will grow and advance remarkably. The general polity surely remains stable and serves the poor and the rich accordingly, and the principles of the ruleof law will favorall irrespective of financial or social, background. The citizens make major contributions in the governance of the society. Everyone develops the right sense of responsibility to contribute positively in the advancement of the nation. But, if the wealth is in the hands of wrong people, the gap of inequality between the rich and the poor in the society will become unimaginable widened. Survival for the fittest will become the order of the day in the society. Somehow, miscarriagement of justice and misplacement of national priority will be inevitable under this unholy romance of wealth and power that be. The most fearful of all, is that militants and terrorist groups will spring up here and there because they appear to be the costumes of the super-rich in an unguarded and corrupt system. This is what account for the massive mayhems on the streets of African nation in the past decades. The worst case scenario on the African streets war at present is the emergence of the assassins without visible armory. He does not engage any lethal force to achieve his mission. His target is your mind. He uses "POWER TOOLS" to work on your and leverages on your peculiar circumstances to take over your mind and control it without a brute force. Well, this work is not some kind of manual to elaborate on the concepts or conspiracy of assassins, rather the main focal point remains – pointing the torch light on advancing African dreams and development realities.

POWER-SUCKERS VERSUS ECONOMIC USURPERS

As the war ranges about who control the government of the people, who control the economy of the state and who controls the minds of the people, the values enshrined within the systems either gets trampled upon or dissolves into oblivion. African does not need some kind of psychic cake-mix to for-tell the obvious future awaiting the continent. It's an established law of the universe, that: "WHATEVER A MAN SOWS, HE ULTIMATELY REAPS". For over three decades now, the continent have witnessed catalogue of leaders of some African States with high profile of technical competence devoid of strength of good character, leaders with good intention to move their society forward but lacks the political will or prowess to deliver on the people expectation, and leaders that have the greatest windows of opportunities to engage development gears but lacked the technical competence to convert opportunities into desired outcomes. The list of poor and corrupt legacies is long and continues to be endemic in the system till date. While some leaders at present are the off shoots of the past administrators, others are group's cloned architecture. Only few African states have right leaders in the public space serving the interest of all.

African is plaque with *"Power-Suckers"* and *"economic-usurpers"* at the party level. In the western nations, political parties have established political manifesto that represents the interest of all in the party, not hand few. If the political party assumes office or takes over power to lead the nation through a free, credible and fair national election, the elected agents must stick to this manifesto and deliver on the people expectation. On the contrast, African politics are filled up with complex interests of people, and not even party interest. Thus, if elected, the agents representing the party become confuse, and rather loot the people treasury.

In a typical African setting, people or group of persons forms some kind of power block to pledge support for a political aspirants on the premise that certain contracts should be given to them or persons from their group. This is short-sightedness, callous and some kind of crime against development. With this kind of development, the elected officials will go into office to service the biddings of such groups and that of the political father for the whole term in the office. At the end of day, individuals gets far richer that the entire nation. The consequences of this wicked practice is implicit as the few-empowered people from the last administration now constitute a major sensitive economic block that controls the influence on the political arena of the next administration. They have the wealth of the people starched away in foreign accounts and in their personal coffers. It's truly difficult to pitch a punch against the "*economic usurpers*". And somehow, the desperate politicians go after them to campaign for support and sponsorship and the next round of the negotiation ensued at the expense of the people's interest. Just imagine the kind of turbo force building up gradually but surely............ it leave one without a word outside the structure "EMERGING OLIGARCHY".

Under this kind of political whirlpool, African do not stand a CHANCE to become one progressive, indivisible and united Africa in the near future not too far on this kind of intelligent re-construction on the political space, the highly esteemed principles of democracy have been crippled permanently and confined to the wheel-chair of antiquity in history. At this point, leadership ceases to be about:

- Competence
- People interests
- Advancement of the society
- Prudence management of resources
- Improving on the state of things in the society
- Improving on the state of the people
- Value creation
- Building stronger ethical institutions
- Raising vibrant society with strong bias for ethics, values integrity and dignity of labour.
- People's interests, people thing.
- Etc.

Unfortunately, this is not some kind of surprise expected in the future, nay; it's already a birth reality on the African shores. Some two decades ago. Take out time to visit the African history gallery in the last two decades, and then, check out the present political matrix and find out about the cascading obnoxious dexterity of the recent political actors and actresses aligning each with their portfolio full of tricks, collabo and antics. On the other hands, check out utterances at campaigns, and other socio-political events, and find out how many times the words: *development, advancement, ethics, value,* and etc., pops up from their mouth. These guys are smart and most atimes employs the services of a Make-believe artist to make appearance most professional to cajole the votes of unsuspecting people.

Some leaders want elongation of terms in the office, even when they lack the legacy of one development adventure in the last administration. Others want to die in the office, and some want the baton of leadership to become a family thing, tribal thing or even a religious thing. Africa cannot get better on this pseudo-political construction, and until politics is separated from the romance of the super-rich and religion including tribal affiliation, African cannot advance to join the rest of the world.

ICEBERG FACTOR DESTROYS THIS KIND OF POLITICAL CONSTRUCTION.

As the water of politics gets dirtier by the incident of this pseudo-political construction, all manners of people join politics and affiliate themselves to different political groups, class and party on a single notion that personal interest is superior to the people interest. Somehow, within the power bloc of each political party; are people whose interests goes far beyond the "Manifesto" of the founding fathers, nay, god-fathers of the party. As the eventsunfolds, this few people uses the tools of money, oratory power and social sophistication to wrestle the group power to their grip and controls the party. At the end of the day, they produce own candidate to become the flag bearer of the political party. Without an air of suspicion, well-meaning individuals in that party will ignorantly sacrifice their integrity, social capital including finance to get a wrong candidate out there on the political space of the people. *They had been deceived by the manifested reality of that professional appearance wore by that candidate*, not knowing the individual they see is but a tip of the ICEBERG of INDETERMINATE ENTITY.

Bingo!! A new government is formed following after the order of the prevalent template and somehow gradually the democratic principles are suspended and its essence demeaned in empirical design of the prevailing operating system. On this juncture, the political class enriches themselves using the legal tools that are entrenched in the system, but on the hand impoverished the people. This kind of political construction uses some media to engage the public with all manners of well managed activities to appear credible and working for the people, while the windmill of most unsuspecting corruption trades on unnoticed. This kind of monster is responsible for the African set back. The cabals keep winning all the time, and the people keep losing all the time. For decades now, this invisible monster has been on the spotlight keeping most African nations in the gulag of under-development, political instability and in comatose of "*failed*" or "*fragile*" State. The political actors/actresses are the ones winning in the real sense, and African dream remain a mere and elusive "Construction of Imagination".

Check out the indices, statistics, facts and figure about African politics just some two decades behind; surprise to find out this monstrous political construction is exactly what has been ripping African apart. Even, when a new political party is formed anywhere, same elements finds a subtle way to impose self upon the party. It's unbelievable that a public servant occupying a political position in the society is not obsessed about building stronger systems and institutions devoid of manipulation, rather busy building up a stage that favors own "ICEBERG" community".

If such constructions are not dismantled from the region political economy, the future of the continent is bleak, fill with woes and irreparable destruction. Imagine what would happen if a terrorist organization succeeded to have one of their own out there on the government corridor of power. Africa will surely boil like Hiroshima under this unholy romance and only time will tell whether African kingmakers have not deep their feet in the bloody waters of regret for this "Pseudo-political Construct". Blank paradox! It's emerging oligarchy!! See the blood in the sky and read the handwriting of the bloody moon. Mene mene tekel prisssss…hhh!!

EVERY CITIZEN OF THE STATE IS A WALKING ICEBERG.

Generally, in real life, each of us represents something far bigger than the manifested quantum reality about us. The truth is that each of represents some kind of content, sign-post, platform, interest, purpose, reality, etc. People relating with us from the point of manifested reality is only dealing with the very "TIP OF THE ICEBERG". What is usually hidden away from the optical eyes is far greater than what we bear on the surface. It is this hidden part of us that at times give the actual information about our true personality. Therefore, in dealing with each person at any time, always think about the huge iceberg submerged in the waters of surprise and uncertainties. This is exactly what makes life a whirl pool of uncertainties.

You cannot tell who is a terrorist from the face. You cannot tell about the one with a heart of gold, brass and bronze from mere empirical analysis or observation of the manifested human. It is difficult to imagine that the beautiful face or the handsome face and soft spoken fellow sitting beside you are the one to detonate the next bomb. Most suicide bombers are really beautiful, speak with soft manners and appear more confident than a normal person. That is the *iceberg factor*. If you only judge by the reality construction of the manifested tip, you will have your titanic ship sink down to the seabed by the unimaginable blow of the force hidden away from your eyes.

The iceberg personality about each of us is not necessarily bad, evil or wicked, nay, not at all. Rather, it takes up personality, and a kind of content that reign supreme in our mind. Its process through the dominant thought in our sub-conscious. This make it important to guard the mind, for out of it – issues of life is determined. Whoever or whatever controls your mind ultimately controls your world. People do not rule over people, rather CONTENT of a personality or CONTENT of CHARACTERof a personality is what rules over people. Thus, whenever an individual wins an election, it's his/her inner election that he/she brings to bear on the office. For instance, if a Lion wins election in the jungle, you do not change its organic reality by pieces of government policy documents and constitution. A leopard cannot change its spot, and a "he-goat" cannot change its smell no-matter the detergent applied. Life is a CONTENT thing. Every one of us is some kind of ICEBERG CONSTRUCTION.

Appearance can be deceitful. Appearance is more of a social construct than a natural construct. Appearance can be design, manipulated and wore on the body like some king of masks or masquerade. If the number of people wearing natural appearances in any given system is outnumbered by those wearing some kind of masks, or "Professional Costumes", the society will be full of issues of various pedigree. From another perspective, if the critical mass of the society (note, youcan put anything here) have their minds governed by value-creation (i.e. CONTENT) and quality selfless vision, then, the society must advance to become their desired dream(s). But, if it is the opposite disaster is inevitable.

For Africa to conquer the ranging inferno of the "Emerging Oligarchy", the people must begin to engage the politicians' space from the iceberg construct of reality about individual and political party reality. Competence is a game of many complex factors either structured or cultured to fit into a reality construct. CONTENT of an individual character should ratherbe a major benchmark to determine who fits into a position before competence come up as a seconder. African will get better, the moment more competent people with true and proven character begin to emerge into leadership positions in the politics, corporate world and sacred institutions. There is nothing wrong with the African soil, climate and vegetation.

To activate the African dream, Africans must be able, willing, and ready to activate the right CONTENT of CHARACTER or MIND to advance. The moment the desire to improve on the state of things and state of people in the society becomes the obsession of the critical mass or block of African population, then, nothing can stop the continent from transitioning into her desired dream. But, if by the way of excuses base upon tribal bias, religious bias, political bias and socio-economic bias – that Africa remain divided in a critical time of her history as now, then, the CABALS will continuously win and the people wind into eventual oblivion. Whatever a man sows, he reaps bountifully.

CHAPTER 3

ARMOURY OF POVERTY:

Poverty is a weapon of mass destruction. Nothing on earth destroys faster like poverty. The most lethal weapon ever invented on the face of earth lacks sophistication, efficiency, potency and efficacy when poverty is involved. Poverty is a scheme; it's a huge business and it is a clear reality construct cleverly designed to put the ordinary people in proper check.

Poverty is the most fearful armory ever invented by mankind.

Poverty is the deadliest Assassin.

Poverty is the greatest killer bomb of all time.

Poverty is the King of all monsters ever created by any government.

Poverty is a HUGE BUSINESS.

Poverty is an intelligent excuse to deceive unsuspecting people.

Poverty is a living organism, call it a MUTANT.

Poverty is not God's creation but man's creation.

Poverty is a fiery armoury that can kill people in mass.

Poverty is the only monster that can DISRUPT a sane mind.

Etc.

7 LIES ABOUT POVERTY

1. Poverty comes upon people as a curse.
2. Poverty is lack of money and material things.
3. Poverty is for people who are physically challenged.
4. Poverty is a spiritual accident.
5. Poverty has nothing to do with an individual's character.
6. Poverty is for the minority group and less privileged in the society.
7. Poverty is the reward for the unschooled people.

7 LIE ABOUT AFRICAN POVERTY

1. Poverty is a must for the color people in every society.
2. Africa is wrongly located, and that is the cause of her poverty.
3. African poverty is causcd by colonialism
4. African poverty is the import of her climatic difference.
5. Africa is poor because the continent lacks major natural resources and minerals.
6. African poverty is traceable to the DNA of her people.
7. African poverty is a curse placed upon colored people by God.

The cause of poverty on earth has been a major debate across the poles of the universe. The real truth that must be told any day is that poverty is a compounded complex issue that can be linked to too many things by different schools of thought. Another truth is that poverty can be conquered by anybody anywhere in the world. Poverty thrives in ignorance, and wherever knowledge shows up; it disappears. The biggest problems of the poor in the society are that- the super-rich trades on the stock of poverty and grow their riches. Poverty is a HUGE BUSINESS for the super-rich, most powerful and super-influential people of the world. The wealth of the earth can go round everybody, but not everybody is ready to pay the price to escape poverty. Riches or poverty is first a choice thing, before it does become a chance thing. It takes having the right choice for riches to engage the opportunities around. A mind without such a decision has already prepared to bath in pitiable poverty ever before it shows up.

The art of scaling up one's meal ticket is in itself is a huge business. The poor and the rich are given same volume of opportunities every 24hrs, but the rich have cleverly acquired the right tools, skill mesh and knowledge to engage opportunities and converts it effectively into desired outcome. The poor have failed to acquire the necessary tools, skill mesh and right knowledge pedigree to engage opportunities effectively. The rich nations of the world have developed economic systems that enable them engage opportunities as they come and turn it into desired results. While the poor nations continuously pass-over-opportunities-without the least due on how to engage opportunities.

An advanced nation spends so much money on research and documentation. The school curriculum of most advanced economics are reviewed regularly to keep it in proper phase with the reality on ground in the nations, curriculum is remains unchanged for decades because the systems have failed to vote enough budget for research and documentation. This school curriculum is a tool destruction of unsuspecting people. It's anthem the most African graduates cannot compete at the global level. This is because most courses in the school curriculum have expired for decades.

Most jobs publications online, oversees and across the world today requires 21st century skill-mesh to secure them. The rate of graduate's unemployment tells a story of lack of requisite job-skills that the available jobs requires. In the budding stage of today super-industrialism, jobs were given to people who came in search for them; but the reality in the employment space at the moment showed that most graduates do not have employability skills. Jobs are now given to people that meets the demands of the job. Its either a graduate go back to school to lead the right course or attend refresher courses to equip him/herself, self-improvement is a must for today's graduates. It's even far better to graduate with a solid business plan and business proposal. That makes you edgy in your professional space.

POVERTY IS A CONTENT THING

Poverty is not really absence of right job opportunities as per se, rather a reflection of lack of right content in people. Opportunity is also a content thing, not a certificate affairs. Most big enterprises, multinationals and public companies around the world are established by unschooled brains. Some are school-dropouts that turned out corporate sellouts. Most of these business gurus do not have one certificate, but have the enterprise cockling up in their minds. They beat the fangs of poverty to nib on their dreams, and the rest is story.

The school curriculum content of most third world nations'are designed by the super-rich or those on the higher wrung of the economy ladder. Little wonder, the schools in Africa appears to produce raw materials for the Western Nations. African supplies the labour force that builds the economics of the most advance economies around the World. In the recent times, more African sons and daughters have migrated to Europe, Australia, United Kingdom and United States of America. This has scaled up brain drain to alarming rate. Unfortunately, most African governments appears to be clueless about what to do exactly to reverse this dangerous trend. In a report published in the month of June, 2015 by one of the leading newspapers in Nigeria- the Spain Ambassador to Nigeria hinted that, about 250 registered Spanish nationals are resident in Nigeria, while on the other and, more than 40, 000 Nigerians registered Nigerians are resident in Spain. In the real sense, that statistics is quiet indicting and pointing some kind of imbalance portrait to Nigerian government.

The followings might be probable reasons for this significant disparity in figures (250: 40,000):

- Political instability
- Poor power supply
- Poor road network development
- Standard of living
- Average life expectancy
- Poor market systems/structure
- Terrorism
- Insecurity of life & properties
- Unemployment
- Poor economic system
- Etc.

On the part of Nigeria, the above listed looms very large in that picture for the disparity. Though the reasons captured so far above is not enough, then, any sane mind can tell for sure that more talented Nigerians, learned, graduates and scientists are living and working in other parts of the world. (Insert Necessary Facts & Statistics here)

The same thing applies to other African nations and third world countries of the world. The host nations are on the receiving sides as their GDP's shots up by the revenue generated by this block of brain-drain.

The African problem cannot be fixed by the diaspora alone, rather Africa leaders need to wake up to challenge this status quo. The continent has what it takes to fix the electricity challenge, build the economy and create massive opportunities, fix the polity, and upgrade the social and road infrastructures. The resources to do just that are there, but the will power to do just that is the actual challenge here. It's either the leadership is ignorant about this or allow the challenges to deepen and degenerate to critical case scenarios.

It appears too often that some leaders are actually using poverty as potent tool to perpetuate state in the office. The people in such society become so poverty stricken that they see themselves as mere slaves before the leadership. In some society, it's a sectarian thing, tribal thing or even worse some kind of cold religious war against certain people. It is difficult for African to develop to anything great beyond the present status quo. A look at the African economic trajectory at the present, it is easy to tell that most economic growth is macro and not micro. The people at the top of the national economic pyramid are consciously protected from the devastating economic crisis of the system. The commoners on the streets have consistent remain the losers in almost every African States. The system is heated up, the policies are made without consulting the people, and many times the ruling forces impose pressures on the people. This usually create some kind of "*survival for-the-fittest-mentality*" on the streets across Africa.

African street are filled up with bloody stories of various kinds and the pile of these dirties keep increasing daily. Funny, the some leaders appears to be clueless or ignorance about this development. Some embark upon projects that do not shop visible and positive impact on the people. Others turns the public office to a sectarian platform to only favor few against the interest of the majority. It's unfortunate that, some development partners do not really know about some of this maverick policies and national misplacement of priorities.

A closer look at some leadership in African soil, one need no soothsayer to tell the end from the beginning of such leadership. It is a development crime, nay, disaster for Africa to vote into office men who are above 70 years into public service space. If an aged soul hasanything to offer to the society, he can do it from the sideways either as a special consultant or special advisor. The 21st century reality is not same as the past 18th, 19th and 20thcenturies. In the world of ideas, creativity and speed, the aged mind can boast of competence, but not outcomes from myriad of opportunity cascading down from the voidat the speed of radar of change. Obviously, leadership is not about "*aged mind*, rather about '*edgy-mind*'. For as thc universe shrinksfurther at the speed of change in computing speed, the entire earth is fast becoming a "*global parlour*". The *aged-mind* is some decay-rate away in ideas whose time has gone since four decades ago.

In most advanced nations of the world, the leaders age is in the range (35-56) and (57-60yrs). The truth is that some entered the public service space much earlier than their present age status. That means, they have grown with realities on ground, and the very attraction here, is that they do not want to die in office as their African counterparts. Some of these folks have different mentality. They believe in servicing the interest of the society and not own interest.

For the Western folks, serving just the peoples' interest and doing it well is enough legacy and satisfaction to live by. Even, with little saving or none, these leaders prefer to be remembered for good and positive impact. This is not common on the African soil. In Africa, some past leaders looted the economic and raped the national coffers clean while leaving the office. It's not my interest to flood the pages of this book with data, statistic, facts and figure. I strongly refrain from doing this because GOOGLE SEARCH ENGINE is already smoldering with such. My focus or core interest in this work is to create a wakeup call to the younger generation to brace up in the place of national transformation or regional transformation driven by unity of purpose, unity of interest and unity of vision. I do strongly hope, that the young people do not repeat the mistakes of the past leaders and neither celebrate the unchallenged works of some leaders in the region.

The poverty ravaging the continent was created, imported and nurtured to its present status quo by the instrument of leadership. It's not the World Bank branding "as third countries' that made the African society poor, rather it is a direct making of the African leadership. As at 1985 Dubai depended on Nigeria Airways operation, but by 2005, Dubai could boast about 200-300 Aircrafts while Nigeria at the moment has non but depend on Arik airways as

National carrier. What really happened? *Poverty is a content thing.*

The picture of any nation at any time is a reflection of the true "content of character" and "personality" of the Leadership at that time. Whatever obtains on the streets of the nation is the actual values or de-values created by the leadership. The Leadership over any society did not drop from Heaven, rather drawn from among the people, thus, people gets the kind of Leadership that suits them at any time. This is not a farce, not magic as per se. if the Leadership of any people suffers poverty of useful ideas, innovative insight and poverty of advancement creativity, it must affect every rank and file of the society. Leadership either builds people or unmakes their true destinies. Every resource in the society can only deliver high productivity, high performance and deliver on people expectation whenever a true/good leaderassumes office. But, the reverse is the case when a corrupt, clueless, ignorant, self-centered, tribalized, and sectarian leader is in the office.

Belief system is a strong factor when it comes to leadership, because everything the leader sees, hears or does filters through the belief system. If the leader's belief system is distorted deliberately or not, the society will suffer untold set back. That's why, when it comes to leadership, competence, good health and certificate works are the least on the scale of importance. The strength of the leader's character or weakness, or even bias is the main focal point. Good character cannot be bought with money, rather must be nurtured over time.

A technically certified competent leader, but has stronger affinity to loot the economy is a development disaster to any society. Corrupt leader is never a blessing to any people anywhere in the world. It's only in the game of negotiation or sport that professional appearance can be worn, but not in more sensitive and sacred issue like leading a state/nation. It's good character and right attitude that keeps a leader in the office. It's an error if the people vote into the public space a leader base on technical competence devoid of strong flare for:

- Accountability
- Transparency
- Due-diligence
- Commendable integrity
- Golden legacy
- Rule of law, etc.

Once the leader is deficient of empirical truth required to drive good governance and build story leadership pedigree, then, the system or society will be bankrupt of strong institutions and strong people of high ethical fibre. It is on this premise that evils will be breed, nurtured and empowered to ravage the society. This is not too far fetch from the reality on ground in most African society. It is the content of the leadership that begets the reality of any people. Also, before any people become poor or suffer financial poverty, character failure of the apex governance most have been pampered for a very long time unnoticed.

POVERTY IS A NEW GOVERNMENT

"If you can impoverish the people using the weaponry of poverty, you force obedience out of them.....then, you surely rule over them, because you can now control their minds" Ritchie Felix..

Poverty is the *assassin* without a scabbard. It's the naked fighter, fury and fierce in battle-field that misses no target. It's more fearful than a plague or Shakespearean witch spell. It is legal weapon of power mongers and the newest government of the 21st century on the streets of Africa including other third world countries. From researchers,it seems that; the more poverty impoverishes the people- the government and the super-rich people gets better, bigger, become more significant and often time, scale up their meal tickets amidst the outcry of the people.

The universities are churning more graduates now than before, and the job opportunities around is not growing at same exponential progression. The streets of Africa are filled up with unemployed youth; both skilled and unskilled. The youth in the age range (18-35) yrs. constitute more than 55% of the African population at the present.

This samebracket represents the economic class of the continent and the future of the region rest upon the energy and knowledge content of this age bracket. In the world of development; any society that empowers this force (i.e. age bracket) has succeeded to create an envious future ahead of her posterity. And any society that gambles with this energetic force has programed disaster in the future. It's this age brackets that accounts for:

- Terrorism
- Assassination
- Cultism
- Gangsterism
- Militancy
- Oil bunkry
- Election violence
- Street wars
- Mafiasm
- Rape-vices
- Prostitution
- Etc.

When the powers of the State or the Powers that be fail to empower this age range positively and sustainably, the future of such society is bleak. The greatest problem of Africa is what her leadership has done with this age bracket since the independence of each Africa State. The people worst hit by the bug of poverty in every African State at moment is the people within this age bracket. The ten poorest countries of the world enlisted by the United Nations are all located in Africa. What future portends for people in this age bracket considering the growing poverty across Africa cannot be described in words. It calls for sober reflection.

Being poor as a youth left the African child without much option than to do the bidding of the *money-bags* in the society. Today, African youth are the ones rigging election, snatching the ballot boxes, community political killings and kidnapping, because they have been paid by some of the big money-wigs of the society. Some cabals in the society even create secret militant camps, terror groups and assassin squads and arm them to the teeth to serve their personal interests. The same force that would have been directed to secure the future for the society, now works for just few cabals at the expense of the entire society. For real, African cannot develop this way or attain her desires in this setup.

My lawyer friend told me how much he tried in a futile attempt to change the mind of a kidnapper that took him hostage for five days. He said, the young man that was in-charge of looking after the camp when others has gone to the field to get more people, confessed that; "as far as there are no jobs available for a graduate or ever for the unskilled,they have to find a way to survive the poverty in the land". And for him, kidnapping is a bomber business innovation on the street. The younger kidnapper further confessed: "as long as they keep sharing the money up there on the corridors of power, we wait to cut our share of the pie from the society in this camp. It's obvious in the African historysome three decades ago, that, kidnapping was unheard of in the land. But, today it's has dominated headlines. It's a business that thrives on the absence of:

- Sustainable job opportunities
- Political stability
- Good governance

49

- Leadership empathy
- Peace
- People-oriented projects, etc.

Whenever poverty is enshrined in a system either consciously or unconsciously, the people in the society develop the *"survival-for the fittest"* mentality. Nothing kills ideas, value creation and profitable enterprise like this poor mindset. No nation ever attains her desired-dream land on the heels of poverty mental syndrome. That is why; it's very difficult to predict great future for African even in the next two decades ahead. This is no curse or attempt to cause fear or even defame the corporate image of the continent. If the TRUTH must be told, then, let's call a spade - spade and not a garden fork. There is need for the African present leadership to wake upon the right-side of the mind, and bid good-bye to:

- Politics of religion
- Politics of sectarian group
- Politics of selected cabals
- Politics of tribal interest
- Politics of militant/terrorist group
- Politics of favoritism, etc.

Leadership or mainstream politics should *be about improving the state of things in the society and improving on the state of the people*. Anything outside this reality is but mere farce, adulterated and a complete disaster awaiting intelligent excuse to happen.

AFRICAN DEVELOPMENT IS STASHED AWAY ACROSS THE ATLANTICS FROM AFRICA SHORES.

No American President, Governor, Senator or any cadre of public service officer own a personal saving account in Africa. Same thing with European and the United Kingdom public saving officers, but African leaders have personal foreign Accounts across the poles of the universe. This money stashed away in Swiss banks, UK banks, Europe banks and American banks represents African development stolen away from its shore. Some leaders do not have the least faith to invest in the country they are serving at the least to give back to the society some dividends from the stolen money or wealth they have accumulated for themselves and for their offspring. This is a RAPE on African people.

How can the potentials of the African market be activated under this high level apathy of the leadership? Rather, African leaders believe that foreigners, oversees grants, aids and foreign investors will develop the African markets, build the needed infrastructure in the society and grow the people standard of living.This is what every African Leaders in most countries have done over and over for decades now. It's a development error that has caused:

- Civil wars in some African state.
- Massive unrest in African society
- Poverty of the highest order on African streets
- Poor social amenities and infrastructures
- Closure of schools

- Destruction of innocent lives
- Electoral violence
- Under-development of the region
- Massive brain-drain
- Massive migrant crisis
- Etc.

America was built by American people.
Europe was built by Europeans
United Kingdom was built by her people
The Caribbean was built by her people
Africa must be built by African people

Even if, all the foreign aids, grants, overseas investors' money including loans from Paris clubs are turn into African shores – it will not build Africa. Money does not build nations rather it is people that build nations. It's not a matter of milling out development documents, rolling out power points from Nigeria to South Africa, and sleeping in meeting from Ghana to Cameroon Sermonizing about white elephant projects. The region has really deactivated catalysts of developments because of some leaders bid to enrich themselves and take wealth abroad.

If 40, 000 plus Nigerians lives in Spain alone while 250 Spanish citizens lives in Nigeria as at June, 2015. Then it means more than ten productive African nations lives in diaspora when you culminate the statistics of other African nationals living across the Atlantic from Europe, United Kingdom, Caribbean and United States. How did Africa come to this status quo, and how can this massive brain-drain be reverse? It's just a biting question that African leaders need to answer.

African nations lost millions of dollars on declined migrant visas daily, yet, visa applications increases exponentially in all the foreign embassies. Most African migrants are turn into silos, prisons and gulags in foreign host nations to rot for life. What are the African leaders doing about this? I really do not want to plunge into statistics because they are not hidden. Google has it all. It is truth, that, African missions abroad handles most of these responsibilities, but the best offer from some of these missions abroad is just a BIG BOLD JOKE considering the budget given to them. Today, more Africans are killed around the world as drug traffickers, prisoners of some sort, illegal migrants and others. Yet, we have Leadership living on the people tax, but doing nothing in the real sense. Well, the fundamental focus of this book is not to critic African leadership rather to wake up some that are REALLY SLEEPING on seat of power.

But come to think of it, why would Africa youths including some adults would want to migrate abroad? Is this not enough story line to indict the governments of their inefficiencies, lack of solution to the problems on ground and gross apathy about tinkering the states toward real development? Is this not telling the people on the corridors of power, that there is so much poverty in the land? Who is cheating who? When you turn on CNN television station, the reports coming from Africa do not point the kind of future people desire in the 21st century. The news content from the region is not inspiring to any Africa teenager living home or abroad, rather makes one to think the other way round to look far away to escape horror. It's a pity that in this 21st century when African States supposed to be on top of the donor nations of the world, African States are still looking out for grants, aids, and loans from Paris club to sponsor her annual budgets. What a development flaw? And to add injury to insults, some leaders still embark on overseas shopping spree, holiday and summer barbecue in the Caribbean's. It's huge error!

When will African turn into tourist destination for Europeans public officers, American Presidents and United Kingdom tourists' attraction? When will an African state come up to construct its society to be like Dubai? When will Africa begin to build stronger institutions with a global character and attraction? Is it that, the continent lack resources or the political will or political character in her leadership to tinker the region towards colossal developments with strong bias for global standard, attraction and character? This is one question every African public servant must answer. The truth must be told now, not someday. The generation of *power-point's leaders* in public office must expire to give room for a generation of *character-points leaders* to move Africa forward.

As at 1980s, the following nations depended on foreign aids to run their national affairs including:

- Spain
- Singapore
- Indonesia

- China
- Japan
- Brazil
- Nigeria
- Ghana
- Sudan
- Ethiopia
- Malaysia
- Cameroon
- Caribbean
- Mali

By 2005, Spain has top the list of highest donor nation of the world, Singapore had emerged into first tier, economic and political advanced nation of the word. Indonesia has become huge economic attraction of the world, China and Japan has emerged into the league of super-industrial economies of the world. Brazil now builds her own cars in commercial abundance and emerged as the tourist attraction of the world despite all her challenges. Malaysia has become world foremost event center, huge market attraction, stable economy and a kind of paradise on earth. But, Nigeria and other African states on that list are still in shameful doldrums still grappling to get their feet on a *"make – believe"* stage theaters, of emerging economics. Withal the natural endowments and human capital domiciled in the region, most African States have failed to deliver on expectation of the World.

CHAPTER 4

BLOOD IN THE CLOUD

At the moment, the worst terrorists' fatality happened here in African soil almost on daily basis. The worst corruption adventure happens here on the African shore 24/7. The greatest population explosion happening right now in Africa, and by 2050, African will be the most populated continent in the world. This means, Africa could boast of being the greatest hub of human capital or labor force by 2035. The world will probably depend upon Africa for massive supply of labour force across the poles of the universe as from 2030. But unfortunately, from the reality check on ground; – is African really prepared for this onslaught? How prepared is the African leadership brass to make this a huge reality. Can Africa boast of having the facility, social capital, leadership pedigree and vision including values-creation to make this happen here in the region? If the African leadership machine lacks the least clue about this emerging reality, then, blood bath is inevitable in this religion. If the population explodes in geometric progression and value creation, strong institutions, integrity grid job opportunities cum strong leadership pedigree explodes in arithmetic progression, then, it is difficult to navigate the African development ship away from visible fatalities. This is not a dream. It's no farce either. The future is already loading before us today, check the news media, the body language of some African leadership and the continuous writing on the *cloud..mene mene tekel pireshhh..!* What is the African leadership doing at the moment to avert this impending doom? Unless the

Africa leadership wakes up, this reality would surely and gradually catch up with us pant-down. What is happening today on Africa streets represents the portrait picture of what is to come upon the land should things continue the way they are at the moment. If the rate at which people graduate from the universities around the region do not match the rate of value of creation. It's fatality on the contrary. It is a development error to breed what you cannot nurture till it begins to make useful and major contributions to the society. It's a crime against development intelligence to create monsters out of innocent and unsuspecting people. Population explosion is a huge blessing and resource for a prepared government and prepared people. But, it turns a bloody spot in the history of unprepared people and government that lack the least clue on what need to be done. Is African leadership mechanism ready for population explosion because the reality is already upon our domain?

TEN EVILS OF POPULATION EXPLOSION WHEN THE SOCIETY IS NOT PREPARED FOR IT

1. Leadership loots the common wealth of the people, corrupt the values of the system and builds corrupt institutions.
2. The society becomes a shopping ground for terrorists and militant organizations.
3. The future of the economic class in the society is destroyed, and their destiny becomes aborted.

4. The system favors power mongers and economic blood-suckers ahead of right people with strong leadership pedigree.
5. Justice is consistently miscarried and the judiciary becomes weak and weaker by day.
6. Politics becomes a dirty game for those who have the gut and could boast of lethal weaponry in their possessions, and have network of evil forces in their support.
7. The society breeds unemployment, poor road construction, poor power supply, poor infrastructure, poor family systems, poor school systems and poor health organizations.
8. The system favors cheat, deceit, incompetence, the unschooled without vision, the rogues, the streets urchins and the power clusters.
9. The system celebrates mediocrity in the open in the place of pursuit for excellence.
10. The best, the most competent, the progressives, the citizens with good intentions are plundered.

THE TEN BLESSINGS OF OVER POPULATION WHEN THE SOCIETY IS PREPARED FOR IT.

1. Excellence is highly prioritized, celebrated and given due progression in all sectors of the society.
2. The judiciary works effectively and efficiently in justice delivery. The judiciary becomes the voice of the people and the hope of the commissioners on the street.
3. The leadership groom leaders with strong ethical fiber, impeccable integrity grid, and delivers on the people mandate.
4. The system builds vibrant and strong institutions that thrives in "due diligence"and "due process" as entrenched in the general constitution of the State.
5. Take-off of medium scale enterprises and growth of the state economy.
6. Security of lives and properties is watchword of the leadership, and is never compromised at any point in time.
7. Advancement of science and technology and activation of super industrial economic build up.
8. Massive creation of intellectual properties, protection of patents and celebration of intellectual properties.
9. Strong and vibrant health care system.
10. Consistent rise in human capital quality and exponential growth of opportunities.

"Terrorism doesn't arise on its own; by identifying the factors associated with it, long term policies can be implemented to improve the underlying environment that nurtures terrorism. The most significant actions that can be taken are to reduce state-sponsored

violence, reduce group grievances and hostilities, and improve effective and community-supported policing."

-- Steve Killela

It is the fundamental assignment of African leadership to identify the prime economic, social, sacred and political factors that aggravates the incidents of terrorism and bloody militancy. Not just identifying these factors, but also device actionable modalities to assuage the aggrieved group(s) and reduce the incessant attack on innocent and unsuspecting citizens of the society. In 2013, 66% of all fatalitiesclaimed by terrorists attacks were caused by four terrorist groups and the worst case scenarios happenedon Nigeria soil. Like I said earlier, my interest in this work is not to show or flaunt to the bare eyes my professional prowess in data simulation, analysis and interpretation, nay, not all. Google search bar is still effective and is awashed with all these statistics, figures, dates, facts and infographics. Rather my unrepentant passion here is to call to consciousness of the upcoming generation of Africa to look beyond the prismof ethnicity, religious affiliation and sectarian politics to dwell on the *"African Dream"*.

Voting more money to procure weapons will not help to fight terrorism on the African soil, rather creating more values in the system, upgrading standard of living and creating the right and enabling environment for all to thrive and fulfill existence will curtail the future uncertainties. If the leadership can make strong investment in raising people of quality and building stronger and vibrant institutions, then the region has hope in the future. Anything short of this is like taking a stroll in the wild jungle unarmed. The ruling powers need to invest more in creating a sane and sound society to discourage upcoming generation from joining militant camps and terrorist organizations.

ON A TYPICAL AFRICAN STREET THERE ARE MORE CONDITIONED REBELS THAN MANIFESTED TERRORISTS

As I write this sub-section, a coup just happened in Bokinafaso, and crisis is rising daily as the people of that African State agitates for and against the development. Whereas, in the Western World; and Asia, technological geeks are breaking through new grounds to shift the boundaries of technological realities. The Asia tigers are fast taking over the global economic attraction of the moment while Africa is simulating policy papers of various pedigree. It's a blank paradox of the 21st century.

On every typical African streets in the region there be more conditioned- rebels than manifested terrorists. Most citizens are not really happy with their governments. Obedience to serve the society is forced out of people because somehow the patriotic spirit has evaporated into the void. More angry people hit the streets daily. Little wonder, every past administrator of some African states uses the service of body guards and hardcore security intelligence to move around. Unlike in the U.S.A- where you can bump into Mr. Bill Clinton or Mr. Obama in a coffee shop. Such cannot happen here in Africa, and that means something is terribly wrong somewhere that need to be fixed properly.

The budget to fight terrorists should rather be directed or its equivalent mapped out to create values, nurture raw talents and turn visions into huge ideals to drive the state enterprise. *The sound of bullets and bombs* cannot really advance Africa towards her desired future dream, rather *sound education* driven by strategic entrepreneurship can change the rather radar of things to favour the region.

I strongly believe that any leader that fails to deliver on his/ her campaign promises or manifesto is a PRIME TERRORIST. A good leader do not need *life-term* in the public office to improve on the *state of things* and on the *state of the people* under his governance. Late Mandela never asked for such to leave a huge legacy for his generation. Great leaders from around the world walk into the place of leadership with unrepentant passion to fix the standard of living. That's pure leadership. It has lot to do with:

- Having *sense of mission*.
- Having *sense of urgency* of that mission.
- Having *restlessness* till *right visions* are turned *into right values* for the people.
- Having the *integrity grid* to serve as the *role model* of the people
- Having the *right* swagger to go against *established criminal enterprises* in the system.
- Having the *right competence* that the job demands of Leadership.
- Having the sensitivity to expand on the right development mechanism and activate unity of interest among the people
- Having the right spirit of sportsmanship, not a do or die attitude, etc.

When a leader builds upon these ethical structures as listed above, the content of state's character surely replicate itself gradually, but surely on the streets. If a leader fail to activate these strategic building catalysts... the story lines from the streets cannot be a miracle. What happens on the streets mirrors the values or content of character that any leader brings to bear on the table of his appointment.

The most important assignment that makes the leader ... the people attraction is *improving on the state of things in the society at large*, not pursuit of things that do not command immediate intrinsic and extrinsic value on the people-space. For the people if a leader fight against:

* Terrorism
* Corruption
* Ghost government workers
* Cyber insecurity
* Gay syndrome
* Gender imbalance, etc.

It's a mere farce. It's too abstract for the people to really celebrate the effort, competence and sensitivity of the leader. People would rather celebrates a leader who can fight terrorism, corruption, ghost government workers and the rest of that list simultaneous with strategic project design, project activation and project delivery that impact on them directly with visible and empirical evidence on the standard of living. People standard of living should not be trampled upon because the government is fighting ghost workers. That is huge error. Good road constructions, upgrading public social amenities and infrastructures across the entire society should not be put on hold because the government is fighting cyber insecurities. That is pure deceit wearing a professional excuse. What is the correlation? Whatever achievement the government can only prove by the use of power-points slides or the walls of media tools, but not have a physical material equivalence for the people to feel it, is but a mere farce. It is pure fiction, and a staged managed error before the people court. The truth is that, the people wants the recovered loot to be used for improving visible state of things around the society. Long paper works corrupts and kills the enterprise of African future faster than any weaponry of the Terrorists.

If every African leader is ready to build good bridges where there was none, build hospital where there was none, create constant power supply where there was none and construct quality roads where there was none, then, the region automatically advances at unimaginable speed to join the comity of advanced economies. But if, the leader fails on these grounds and continue with cheap excuses in the media---------what would come out of the streets of Africa in the near future not too long from now will rain blood from the sky. The bloody cloud is gathering at every point of misplacement of national priority. A hungry man is a conditioned rebel, and a graduate without a job opportunity, is a potential recruits of either militant camp or terrorist organization. A saying goes like this, "when the desirable is not available, the available becomes desirable."

☐ MADNESS OF NIGERIAN ECONOMY AT THE MOMENT

Africa will not advance significantly without the economy of the most populous black state of Africa-Nigeria. For 16yrs ago, the country have had democracy in consistent practice, much have not really advanced considering the degree of available opportunities that seemingly surround her economy. On the paper the country is dubbed by some financial institutions around the world as the 20th largest developed economy in the world at the moment but this claims are yet to materialize in the living standard of the people of Nigeria. The advance in macro-economic strength is yet to be equaled at the micro-economic realities.

More than 60% of Nigerian citizens actually live below $2.00 on daily basis. The apparent celebrated growth of the economy appears to be an exclusive reserve of the super-rich, the political class and the average economic class of the country. The common man on the street is yet to tell a better story about Nigerian economy. Between 1999 and 2015, Nigerian leadership mechanisms have really advanced in policies, job committee creations, job policies "point's agenda" and transformational quagmires woes. Much has been stolen away from the people treasury and much more still disappears daily in different camouflage. As I write this paragraph my mobile news alert for the day has the following reports:

☐ Construction industry offloads 60,000 workers
☐ NNPC shut down 500 affiliate retail platform and terminated 10,000 jobs.
☐ Importation economy is threatened, and gradually shutting down.
☐ More woes expected as federal government enforces "single treasury account (STA).
☐ Etc.

The ruling party in the country is yet to come up with a functional economic plan for Nigerian people. Investors are crying widely and there is too much pressure on the streets of Nigeria. The enforcement of "single treasury accounts" by the federal government will actually check money laundry, corruption investing capital flight of Nigeria. Equity but on the contrary increase pressure in the labor market, discourage take off infant industry and eventually cause unprecedented lay off not only in the financial institutions but also in all other sectors of the economy. Already, newspaper headlines are awashed with painful happenings. After more than 100 days in the office, in the new regime...democracy is yet to deliver on the people expectations across the states of the country despite the seeming opportunities hanging around. The state governors of some states are lousy acquiring "this" and "that" and scratching various projects just to keep the face up. This is error, if not well dressed development disaster.

Nigeria has all the economic potential to be best economy in the "A"-class, but corruptions of public officers have swallowed that opportunity. If the GMB led anti-graft war against corruption progresses undistracted, there is BIG HOPE FOR NIGERIA. And also, if the federal government of Nigeria can go beyond the last administration under President Good luck Jonathan with the anti-graft war against corruption more loot will be recovered. Another important dynamics that calls for important review by the present administration under General Mohammadu Buhari (RTD) includes:

* Policy about 'Single Treasury Account'
* Power sector contracts since 1999
* Roads construction award since 1999
* Agricultural sector
* Health sector

> * Job creation/national health policies etc.

Obviously, the Nigerian political and economic spaces are both over heated at the moment, except something genuine and relevant is done, 'survival for the-fittest-syndrome will set in, and streets war is inevitable. At least government polices no matter how well – intentioned should empower people and build more vibrant systems, not the very opposite.

Nigeria as a growing economy has grown past where road construction is still a bet in the political game. Nigeria want upgraded standard of living, peace not conditioned cease fire, job creation alongside with value creation, not just anti-graft war against corruption. The Nigerian people want to know and feel how much the leadership in all sectors cares. For every Nigerian has right for:

- For 24hrs power supply
- To know what constitutes the major priories of the federals states government at any time
- To exercise full fundamental human rights
- To contribute positively to the advancement of the economy
- To know about the state and federal government budget
- To live peacefully with each other irrespective of tribe, political affiliation and religious attachments
- To access justice, and given fair hearing in a lawful court as when necessary
- To criticize the government of any level as enshrined in the national constitution, etc.

Nigerian state remains most strategic catalyst in the reconstruction and advancement of Africa in 21st century. It's a huge gain for the Nigerian leadership to make this happen for Africa by unleashing the potentials within her domain and activating the Nigerian economy to its fullest potentials. But if the ruling powers that be at the moment, however, fails to deliver this expectations, it is possible the rest of Africa migrate to join the league of advanced economies while Nigeria wallow in her own mess.

RANDOM SHOKING REALITIES & TRENDS INNIGERIA AT THIS MOMENT

- Nigeria has the highest number of skilled young people in the sub-Sahara.
- Nigeria has the highest number of unskilled young people in the sub-Sahara, and in the world.
- Nigeria has the highest number of young people enrolled in militia camps, kidnapping and terrorist organization in the sub- Sahara.
- Nigeria has the largest labour force unengaged in the sub-Sahara Africa.
- Nigeria has the worst and highest number of violent carnage and terrorist fatalities in the whole world at the moment.

- Nigeria has the greatest investment potential in the sub-Sahara, especially, under the President Jonathan's led government. Despite that, APC led junta might hit up with a more bogus economy advancements as its economic might is taking up so many abandoned projects.
- Nigeria population is exploding exponentially yearly
- Nigeria has the power generation capacity to feed the entire sub-region if fully activated. If the APC government can consolidate on the success triggers of the last regime under President Jonathan in this sector.
- Nigeria economy has the economic potential to outperform china, USA, Britain, France and attars if fully activated
- By 2035, 75% of labor force coming out of Africa will be traceable to Nigeria.
- Nigeria has most arable soil in the world
- Nigeria is the largest supplier of raw cassava in the sub-Sahara
- Nigeria has more people with first Degree than the Great Britain
- Nigeria has the largest number of graduate unemployment in the sub-Sahara.
- Nigeria has the largest number of her best brains in diaspora.
- Nigeria has more number of young people in foreign prisons in the sub-region.

- Nigeria has the greatest agricultural production potential in the whole of sub-Sahara Africa.
- Nigeria is enlisted among the top ten terrorist nations of the world, etc.

  Nigeria's problem is not Islam. Nigeria's problem is not Christianity. Moslems built Dubai and the United Arab Emirate economy. Christians built many Nations around the world.

  Nigeria's problem started with colonialism, and continued with neo-colonialism and still being perpetuated with colonial mentality of some leaders past and present. Until, the people see the BIG PICTURE of one united, progressive and indivisible Nigeria, the center as pictured, in the words of epic novel of late, Professor Chinua Achebe. "CANNOT HOLD".

AFRICAN POLITICS OF APATHY

The key word in the sub-section is APATHY. It has its origin from the key word apatheia, from apathes without feeling. This means lack of feeling or emotion (impassiveness) and lack of interest or concern (indifference). According to Merriam Webster dictionary of the 21st century; the base of African political and economic setback is the politics of apathy. People emerge into the public service space without the least concern, interest and strong passion to really activate the process, systems and catalysts that will stimulate advancement for the benefits of all.

Some leaders that have emerged into the leadership spaces across many African States wooed people vote on the promise and camouflage of people's interest at heart. But, as soon as they took oath of office, they make switch to an own disguised interest.

It is appalling that most policies of some African leader'sfavors personal interest ahead of people interest. It is difficult to stimulate any economy to attain height and advancement under pressure of politics that favours more the service space than the served-space. The people in the serving space gets

* The better part of the national budget
* The immunity – clause as the national budget able to perpetuate stay in power.
* Bigger and outrageous salary, impress, security vote, and other allowances.
* The lion shares of the national cake.
* Better health budget than the people they serve.
* Etc.

Often, it appears to me that, politics or governance is the biggest business with return on investment (ROI)in town in every typical African society. Al-gore left office with less than $2million and made real wealth from his climatic crisis documentation. But, in the African society, it is as if some leaders are voted into office to enrich themselves, their family members, friends and selected groups. This remain a dangerous curve in the trajectory of Africa development or bid for economic advancement. In some African States, leaders gradually rape the national treasury and leave the national coffers either empty or poorer for no reason. To cover up the mess, most leaders insist on having one of own protégé succeed him. Unfortunately, some of them still succeed to plant a "Development Poison" as a successor. What a development crime?

Once the desire to improve on the state of things in the society or state of the people ceases to be a leader major obsession, prerogative and priority, disaster is unavoidable in most cases. African people are becoming more politically informed and exposed now than in the past. The African economic classes are growing in political knowledge, and have this understanding that right leadership is the TRUE catalysts to actualize the AFRICAN DREAM.

Some leaders do not know that wrong policy is a potent bullet to destroy major opportunities in the state. Any policy that do have immediate or future impact on the people is better described as A SWORD OF DESTRUCTION. A good leader who is an ardent democrat or even republican should know that leadership is all about provident management of things and people within a specific time interval following a well-designed program or vision with measurable outcomes. Leadership is not about dirty politics, deception of people, enriching a selected group or grooming a state of emergency here and there. Leadership is not an excuse to favor religion, tribes, friends and family.

Leadership is not about imposing limitation on all or selected group of people. Leadership is far bigger than any of the above listed. Any leader, that pursues after own interest while in the service space is a blatant BETRAYAL of the State's Trust. Some ambitious leaders, use own Construction Company to handle state's major projects/contracts. It's a huge development crime.

A true leader should be concerned in building the entire society, not some selected parts of the society. Or some selected party's constituencies. Even, handle major projects in states where they did not win any vote under the control of the opposition party. African leaders need to come to term with what constitutes theoriginal tenets of democracy. Any government that must do well have good and formidable opposition party. The main interest of the rulingparty and opposition party should be the same. That interest must be improving the state of things and people in the society. There is nothing like the winners takes it all in the Western Politics. All democratic values must be followed up, invoke into play at all time and for everyone. Nobody is above the law. If the interest of the people is the main obsession of the leadership, then the people must be regularly consulted in a matter that affects them directly or indirectly. There is no room for *sacred-cow* treatment or *specialist-syndrome*. The law of passion, empathy and democracy demand that the people or persons be consulted before imposing policies on them.

In true leadership or democracy, policies should represent the people's interest and not the opposite. African leadership or society suffers untold setback because of gross apathy of the leadership and total neglect of the people challenges. It is insult on intelligence to impose policy on people without first consulting them for approval. It's even a bigger injury on democratic values when the leaders show no respect on people when they question government policies.

CHAPTER .5
LEADERSHIP STRATEGY VERSUS DEVELOPMENT STRATEGY

The reality structure of any given society is determined by the prevailing cultural reality in practice by the mechanism of leadership of the people. This prevailing reality can be the summation of the leadership thought, views, ideologies, interests, missions, objectives/subjective major and minor priorities in short and long term for the society. It is this balkanization of the government's affinity that eventually enriches the most prevailing cultural or augmented reality on the streets of the society. It even pre-empt, pre-program and pre-conditions the 'citizens' minds for or against REAL development in the society.

The streets can shop the best platform and catalysts for dreaming a nation's economy following a common nationally defined interest and objectives or become the zone mindless hostility with prevailing use of brute, lethal and naked forces to dismantle the primary elements, structure and cultural liabilities that engenders for positive development in the society. This is no permutation; the universal law of Karma states 'whatever you sow, you reap' it is the prime assignment of the leadership institution of the state to articulate in bold letters the leadership interest, mission, objectives and strategies as well as the development structure, culture and strategies before her people. This alone precipitate some level of balance in the system, and set up the default interface for the government, people and resources of the state to inter-relate with specific objectives.

When the government fails to separate political strategy from diplomatic strategy, and economic strategy from development (i.e. advancement) strategy, the system becomes among, house heading nowhere. The worst case scenario happens when the political team in a nation's public office comprises to achieve personal aggrandizement.

Development of vital initiations, economic structures and social infrastructure automatically become compromised at the expense of the people.

African leadership institutions remain the most important elements in designing the state's policies and aggregating the best strategies to attaining to set objectives of the society and development strategies is not exclusive. It is the prerogative of the leadership to use the most suitable tactics or operations are devoid of art of violence, damage, corruption, devaluation of life and on the general state of things and people in the society of the state should not undermine development strategy for any reason perceived or articulated. It is the duty of the leadership to continuously keep the governing strategy in same phrase as the development strategy. Anything that bridges this linear operating system or strategic of the state either destroys the composite functions of the state capabilities or de-natures the constituted structure for the state's advancement. Personal interest is one out of many spoilers that can undermine this sensitive relationship.

AFRICAN LEADERSHIP STRATEGY BANE OF AFRICA STREET WAR

Geniality in the sovereignty of states does not in any sense guarantee or signifies in military might economic brilliancy, technological development, institutional capacities and human capital capabilities of states. Each state differs from others on the capacity of TRINITY OF DEVELOPMENT. Every state is composed of the trinity of development: the people, the leadership and the resources of the state. On the platform of creation; all people, tongues, color and race are given equal opportunity by mother nature, but outcomes varies depending on what each people uses to engage the perceived or manifested opportunities. What really constitutes the tool of engagement can be tangible or intangible and can be summed up as "TACTICS".

Africa has equal opportunities as the Western nations including Europe and all other advanced Economics, but commands different outcomes because of "strategies". Every Nation strategies issues from her peculiar policies and the state's policies reflect the true content of the faulty of leadership. Policies are the aggregation of the leadership or people interest.

Whatever the leadership or people decides to be the priority of the state automatically becomes the policy of the system, and it is the responsibility of the government to mold strategies that can enable the implementation or actualization of the state's objectives. Thus, if the policies are faulty, the best strategy that the state can offer is faulty as will.

Outcomes of opportunities are based upon the paradigm realities of state's policies and strategies. If the policies are faulty, the strategies are also faulty and the most component faculty of leadership becomes most disgraced emperor of the state. It is important to issues here as follows.

* **POLICY**: In a democratic setting, policy should be drawn from among the people or their representatives with clear conscience, transparent intent and with obvious basic objectives of improving the state of things and people at the center. It is unethical for the state's marksmen to abandoned the dear articulated policies to impose an own policies on the people.

Once the people's policy is compromised at the apex of governance, then, the state's strategy is biased as well and the outcome of this theaterof distrust is terrible.

Most African leaders runs their own policies once sworn into the office, and this sincerely mark the beginning of failure in leadership. Such personal policy is prioritized at the detriment of the entire society. The fundamental elements of people driven government are suspended directly or indirectly just to make room for the imposed policies go through. It is this kind of leadership maneuver that breeds monsters and landmines on the streets. It is this kind of political reality that creates civil unrest, violence, fragile state, unproductive economy and uncertainties in the future. African leadership faulty policies create faulty strategies and faulty institutes in the society.

* **STRATEGY:-** Refers to the state craft, intelligence, intent, economy, policies, technology, psychology, ideas, knowledge and ideals that are deployed by the faculty of leadership to actualize the state's policies (the basic objectives, subjective, goals). In other word, strategies pre-empt or preconditions the structural and cultural realities of the environment for actualization of the stated or declared policies.

It is the strategy of the government that determines the "risk" present or representative society. For instance, in some parts of the world women are forbidden from wearing trousers. A visitor or tourist (i.e women) must obey the law of the state once she enter such temporary.

That is just one example out of many in different part of the world. Some African leaders have traditional civil background, so that is exactly what they bring to bear if voted into the public space to serve. Othershave military background, and also probably bring the military thing to bear on the public space. Though discipline can help a man to make a swift lift from military attitude to civilian attitude. But this is not always easy; it requires clear conscience, and conscious effort to make that happen.

One of the real challenges facing African leadership is the inability to depend the core values, beliefs and tenants of democracy while in the office. Leadership is not just about sniffing out policies and baking up strategies, it is also expected to expand values and freedom.

* **TACTICS:** Tactics is the crucial element of any leadership in attaining basic goals and objectives. It is the catalyst that bridges the gap between policies and

strategies. A leader fails whenever policies and strategies. A leader with good intension, good plans, and well-articulated policies and well refined strategies can still fail to deliver people's expectation if he commits a tactical blender in the course of implementing a policy or engaging a strategy. Most African leaders fail to deliver on expectation because of tactical blender. Brilliant strategies and well-refined policies can be ruined by poor tactics despite quantum of reflective passion to do otherwise.

For Africa to witness a kind of seismic shift in political and economic realities, REAL tacticians need to emerge into the place of power. Policies don't implement it, rather a tactician does. Strategies don't engage itself, rather a tactician does. A good tactician as a leader will attain heights and break beyond limits, then, set a new record of performance in leadership. Africa needs tacticians now than before.

DEVELOPMENT STRATEGY

Political strategies actualize political goals and objectives economic strategies actualize economic goals and objectives development strategies actualize development goals and objectives.

It's glaring that African states are far from setting real development goals nay, strategies.

In the world of advanced economics; there is a focal point called "DEVELOPMENT STRATEGIES" or ADVANCEMENT STRATEGIES" The spectrum of stratagem involved here radiates with a glowing diplomacy as its core value. It is not a function of paper work, neither an import leadership razzamatazz. Development strategy must issue from the core values, belief system and totality of content of the machinery of leadership.

Some leaders, prefers internal development (that is, vertical advancement) to external development (that is horizontal advancement). It's believed that attaining self–sufficiency is for more appreciated than inter – dependency with others. Some leaders prefer the former while others prefers the later. Little wonder, some continues are really hostile and do not do much in diplomatic relationship with others. These countries do not have favorable immigrant laws, favorable investment conditions to attract external players into own economy and charges so much on import duties. It's real difficult to stimulate such economy in the face of adverse economic or political condition. It is the people that usually suffer major setbacks at any point of crisis whether economic or political. The ruling class are usually immured from the happenings in the society. The best in this kind of political setting suffers untold injury and setback; while the rest are forced to dance the macabreTonga just to either earn a living or stay relevant in the system.

COMPOSITION OF DEVELOPMENT STRATEGY

To activate growth, and thorough advancement of any society, the machinery of leadership has vast responsibilities to play. It is not a wishy–washy trip of the figment of imagination. First, the nation need to identify what constitutes 'Risk' or carry out some kind of risk assessment of getting involved or not getting involved with an – external body. The second thing to do, is to evaluate degree of "identified risk" and strong possibility of clear cut fatalities. The third thing to do, is to find out what extend the nation has empirical capacity to 'contain' with either 'risk' or 'threat' and is not just about watching at possible intent of external aggression, but also, discovering the capabilities of any perceived adversary. The fourth thiong to do is to come up with strategies to ward off or conquer any external aggression that would likely make the basic objectives to become counter-productive.

On this very note, development strategy is encompasses 'risk assessment' of the intent to get involved in growth, advancement or expansion of opportunities around, the people, the government and the resources available or perceived to available. For instances, a nation embarking on the mission to procure military ornaments, technology and might at the expense of the nation's economic development especially, when it is obvious that the be no threat within and without is a huge error.b a pure development strategy must have a pure philosophy not codified. It must be smart and must be detailed in its missions and objectives. By being "SMART" it means:

a) S= It must be specific in goal-setting and its mission outlook.

b) M= its 'input' and 'output' must be measurable.

c) A= It must be attainable, not fictitious. Its imperative, to declare and detail every bit of the 'process' and 'Engagement'.

d) R= It must be 'reliable' such that everybody getting involved in its implantation knows from ambition what consequences to expect as outcome.

e) T= It must work with a specified time bound. The people must be able to tell when to expect outcome, where to expect, what to expect and how.

It's wrong, if not a crime if it is only the government can tell when to expect the outcome of a strategy, especially, if it is economic strategy. As long as democracy is concerned, the government is there to represent the people and not a people. The axles of development can become grounded when governance become autocratic or a tool to actualize few people's interest at the expense of that consensus. There is no person who is bigger and better than them the rest in any society. Thus, it is a wise thing to carry everybody along even in the midst of challenges. It is the government with the people that weathers through challenges not the other way round.

CLOG IN THE AXLE OF DEVELOPMENT

In a situation where all the arms of government are working effectively and efficiently in the society, it is called "LINER OPERATION STRATEGY". Everybody in the branch of the government in this system operates from its original sense of mission objective of organization and strength of capacity. On the other hand, in a situation, that it is only some selected parts of the government appears to work 'effectively and efficiently'. It is said to be: "LOOP OPERATION STRATEGY". In a typical society, where 'linear operation strategies' is the approach to moving the entire system toward advancement, the government keeps the people support, maximize and optimize the resources deployed to make strategy happen. Everything in such system naturally progresses to set basic standards. Through the speed might be probably slow, it is the best approach to massive transformation.

However if the system uses 'LOOP OPERATION STRATEGY', the development/ advancement attained might be strategic, but the following realities cannot be avoided:

- ☐ Government is satisfied, but the people are not.
- ☐ Some parts of the government develop a sense of superiority when it is not even necessary.
- ☐ Competition sets in rather than complement.
- ☐ Government eventually become unstable and probably fails in the near future.
- ☐ "Its own thing-syndrome" sets in and cripples the axle of progress.

It is against this backdrop that the thesis of this book centers on the fact that the war on the African streets is a bye-product of the government of the society at any time. "Loop operation strategy" has not really helped Africa to unleash her true economic potentials. It has created monsters, damages, violence, corruption and unending fatalities at its best. It's a huge development flaw:

Where the President of a Nation works with Federal Senators at the expense of the State Governors.

Where the governor of a state only recognizes the forces from his party and work in complete disdain of other forces from the other political parties.

When the head of state of a Nation operates a "bulldozer mentality "as Mr. Know it all and Mr. Fix it-all even when progress is not in-view.

Where the State Governor uses building company to carry out road construction network.

Where the people are not consulted until a full blown policy that affects them is implemented.

Where the government works with superrich at the expense of the people.

Where the police works for the government at the expense of the tax   payers' money.

Where the economy favors only the super-rich, the government officers at the apex, government loyalists and the mightiest in the society at the detriment of the people.

Nothing destroys opportunities like ignorance and over-confidence. The trip to the desired destination in the future is simply

ATTITUDE, NOT COMPETENCE. The African chance to secure a golden platform in the future the comity of advanced economic is located with the framework of attitudinal change. There must be a seismic shift of the leader. Over the years, this opportunity has been lost to:

- ☐ Over-confidence of leadership
- ☐ Over-competence of leadership
- ☐ Over-zealousness of leadership
- ☐ Over-sight of leadership
- ☐ Over-softness of leadership
- ☐ Over-laziness of leadership
- ☐ Over-deceit of leadership
- ☐ Over-weakness of leadership
- ☐ Over-smartness of leadership
- ☐ Over-trust of leadership
- ☐ Etc.

There have been strategic opportunities in the past for so many African States to advance into the league of established economies, but retracted back to status quo due to any of the above stated development flaws. African leadership challenges do not really bother on competence, vision, strategy or timing, Or on either "operational art" or "Tactics" use in engaging opportunities. Over-confidence or kind of bulldozer mentality destroys opportunities clinically and holistically. An old adage says; "absolute power corrupts absolutely". This is pure truth! Over-confidence, over-competence and over-zealousness corrupts completely and permanently.

Another major deference to African development or achievement is the leadership guest to elongate term in the office. Some leaders start from day one in office to scheme for a second term, third term or even life term in the office. In most cases, it is a game of bloody business. The leader begin to watch hunt possible opponents or adversary that could stand on his path to achieving his quest. This selfish quest has caused undue damage, have destruction of lives and property in the society. Looking at the whole game at times, it is difficult to point at one thing that leader is doing to profit the society or advance it towards high capacity development. It is short- sightedness of such leaders that has impoverished the African society over and over again. The African political economy history is awashed with catalogue of leadership crimes, gimmicky and corruption predicated upon the quest to perpetuate stay in power.

This selfish scheme to elongate stay in office is what influences the state policy, strategy and tactics of governance. Outside the Late. Nelson Mandela regime, and few others so many African leaders has not really cut selfless vision while in the office. During campaign, they makes loads of promises, and hire professionals to develop convincing manifestation to woo the people votes. As soon as they get into the office, everything become history. They do their bidding, and satisfy own self. That is what has kept Africa where she is today.

When the state's policy is bent to service selfish interest, the strategy of governance at its best and peak is wholly faulty no matter the media demonization about it. It is the people mandate that is raped, and interest trampled upon by the government. Unfortunately, some African heads of State want to die in the office even when it is obvious they are not delivering the right expectation of the people. Others uses the state resources to groom insecurity so that the people live in apparent fear of vicious elements that comes after anyone that dares to challenge the powers that be. For such leaders, he has successfully brought the entire society on their knees. The self-ambitions leader becomes the lord of the rings, a tyrant through in democratic overall, and a specialist of some pseudo-maverick arts within the state. This is society what inhibits the advancement of most African states in sub-Sahara region.

AFRICAN LEADERSHIP IS BECLOUDED BY IMPERIALISM MENTALITY

The imperial masters did not rule Africa with a development plan that can benefit the people either directly or indirectly. It is not that, they lack due about what to do, to activate growth and radical advancement of the African economy. Rather, these folks lack right passion to create the catalysts that will ultimately lead to African hibernation. Their actions and inactions were purely governed by this faulty strategy to keep the people in perpetual slavery.

It's unfortunate that after many decades of imperialism that African leadership still tinker within the circumference of this uncanny reality.

Though some Leaders have really made progress and lifted beyond this reality, many are still drown to their heads in the ocean of imperialism. In the heat of 21st century mill of technological breakthroughs, political evolutions, African, nay, Some African states remain bedeviled with myopic leadership. At a time, when the advanced economics are sealing up their economics into the new any ", most African countries are still divided along the lines of:

- ☐ Ethnic politics
- ☐ Religious politics
- ☐ Sectarian politics
- ☐ Mafia politics
- ☐ Cabalistic politics
- ☐ God- Fatherism Politics, etc.

It is impossible for Africa to get to the land of her dream dressed in this dangerous garments. Ethnic politics creates monsters and bloody serious at its best. Religious politics retards the catalyst of advancement of any nation. Sectarian politics is a huge political error that breeds disasters at its peak.

Mafia politics is destructive and breed the radical that destroys intelligent and well-meaning citizens of the state. Cabalistic politics inhibits growth of any society despite its potentials for something better. God-Fatherism politics remains a political holocaust any day.

Imperial politics seeks for own interest and not the people interest. The society under this leadership interest. Every policy in the society favours the machinery of leadership at the expense of the people. At best, imperial politics can be reduced as politics of a group interest, not state's interest. A closer look at most African states politics, one do not need a soothsayer to tell that, the leader or the leadership is configured to suit the interest of a group and not that of the masses. It is easy to pick out this development inhibitors in the framework of state's policies template is the bane of many African gnomic woos in both politics and economy respectively.

While the government of the day-enters office via credible, free and fair election, the politics, strategies and tactics of governance it employs at work lacks the least anatomy of credulity, free of selfishness and fair to no other people them self. This is a development crime, Error and democratic mismatch at best intelligent construction. If Africa continue to vote for ethnic politics, religious politics, sectarian politics, mafia politics, cabalistic politics and God-Fatherism politics, those more fatalities awaits the continent bigger than brazen terrorism. This imperial master's political mastermind is what continue to create wars, violence and fears on the African streets till date. The region is get to think as one people in real practical terms. Blank misdemeour!

CHAPTER 6
DISRUPT YOUR
GOVERNMENT

The biggest government in town is not the street politics, ethnic politics, mafia politics, and ethnic politics, and religious politics, cabalistic politics and God-Fatherism politics; it's called: "you – GOVERNMENT

INC". Every type of politics is a form of government in disguise whether it has structural reality or not, it is an ideology started by someone, spread by another and keeps expositing by the day. Even the politically elected government might not be there for you rather for a group interest whether visible or not. The only way to survive on the African struts is to make discovery of your own government that no one ever told you till you till now. Even, the school system's curriculum is structured in such a way, this government is never awaken in you all the days of your life. Therefore, at best conscious or subconscious level your mind is programmed to obey rules of the government at the Expense of the "BIGGEST GOVERNMENT" within you.

Whenever you have stop in life is a CHOICE. The prevailing reality hanging of your life is the function of the government at work in you. But, you can really grow bigger better and faster than where you are. The truth is that you need to identify the government that has kept you where you are and do things you do. Identify it now and DISRUPT YOURSELF. The Government berthing within you is the government of your IDEAS, CHOICE AND RULES. That's exactly the government you need to DISRUPT SIMPLE!

DISRUPT YOUR IDEAS

So long you allow the political ideology of the government of the day influence your overall idea about your life itself you are simply caged on all parts of life. You cannot really beat the bangs of reality curve on the streets because the same ideological template running the entire system in the society is the same one running the deep stated resource recess in you.This has literally influence everything about you, your belief, core values, ethical reality and cultural values. Your inner parlance within you resonates at sonic frequency as the vibration of the entrenched reality of the society.

This is why so many people on the streets wants to make it in life at all cost, and at all possible and available means some people are ready to kill to make it. Others are ready to destroy the social values so soiling its pays off at the end of the day. And still, there be a school of thought that believes so much on following due process, due intelligence and ethical codes of the society to satisfy them and contribute to the government of the society.

The truth be told: "it is in the advancement of individual thought pattern, thinking quality, values and cultural realities, that, the society, as a whole advances". If the critical mass of the society population advances in value creation, unavoidably the society advances too. African State suffers unimaginable setbacks and untold hardship because the critical mass of influencers advances in the wrong direction or on the wrong assignment (i.e. priority). It's a serious inhibitor dogging the wheels of progress.

The ideas prevailing over your mind is the real "Government" stepping you from advancing as a person. To break into the next level of your life or become your dreamed self, you need to: "blow out" from the negative social construct that becloud the minds of every average adult on the street. You need to de-construct this prevailing negative pattern running your life, and re-inverts your valuesparadigm.

This is exactly what I call "self –disruption" until you disrupt this poisoned personality berthing deep within you, you sincerely end up like every other person in the society. Do not forget what I shared in the chapter two of this work, that every society is pre-programmed by the prevailing "THINGKING" or "CONTENT" liability of its government.

You really can shift the boundaries of realities around you, and enthrone your own government of creativeand positive ideas. Your ideas is the only potent arsenal (that can give you the stage to change your community for good following established ethical conduct. The government of your ideas has the capacity to immune you from the monster ruling over the society. How? You can decide not cheat , kill, rape, deceive, take bribes, tell lies, and get involved in anything that under mines universal values and human lives. This is timely possible, if you can "DISTRUPT" your wrong ideas, "BLOW OUT" your faulty value parading and "DE-CONSTRUCTION" every poisoned social structures are affiliated to. Just disrupt your government.

12 THINGS YOU NEED TO KNOW ABOUT VALUE – BUILDING IDEAS

1. Ambition can make you accept evil in the place of good, but value- lawing idea makes choose to build a strong future from the scratch

2. Ideas makes you create your own income system amidst devastating plight plundering the society within the prevailing ethical codes in the market place.

3. For you to advance your community against all odds, value- building idea must become your sovereign dictator, and not what obtains on the streets.

4. If you are going to change the world, value- building ideas make become your fundamental arsenal.

5. If you are going to win over blacking on the street, make value- building idea the headquarter of your thought.

6. Nations advances on the weaponry of value- building ideas, and not on military stratagem.

7. Value-building idea is indefectible revolutionist of all time.

8. Command an army of value-building ideas and they will put a desired meal ticket on your table.
9. Your worth in life is relative to the value- building idea that you contribute in the society.
10. Your certificate giveyou job and your value-building idea give you satisfaction.
11. Politics devoid of "Due value-building idea is a naked force or assassin unleashed upon the people.
12. Value- building idea is invaluable strategy that wins everywhere on earth no matter the odds.

THE idea you operate determines the kind of work you do how you does it and where you do it. One value – building idea can deliver huge intellectual properties, and put you in the eye of the market that need you. The idea you operate informs the strategy that you employ at work. While so many people work for just personal consumption, many others thinks about feeding an entire nation. Therefore, one group works for subsistent needs and another works on commercial needs. This two groups has different mentality and different economic paradigms. It is difficult to become super rich along subsistence work or working like a monkey jumping from tree to tree. That is what so many poor people does-jumping from one salary job to another. The kind of work you do determines your monthly output. Yourstrategy to amass wealth is simply poor. The super rich floats a conglomerate and work without salary at th building stage and after some time, wealth begin to follow him

DISRUPT YOU CHOICE

Not everyone can really do the work of the super rich in the society, because anyone can disrupt his or her choice in life at anytime. While the school certificate cannot do much outside salary economy your personal choice per time can.to work as an employee is a personal choice. Even with a Ph.D. certificate you can be a BIG RAT in a rat race. Being a BIG RAT cannot make you feed the nation, but only your family. A Big rat is not necessarily a super rich person in the society, rather only a big wig in a rat race. But, a BIG RAT can be a super rich over might if you dare "DISRUPT YOUR CHOICE" about what you with your life. It's simply a game of switching from fishing from Life Rivers of opportunities without a certificate to fishing with a cottage industry. Disrupt your choice, and create more innovative way to access wealth from universal chest..

Choice begets chance. It's the quality of your choice that separates you from equals or put you under your equals. No matter the strategy, of the government of the day, your choice sets you apart and gives you freedom. Government policies and create your desired world. Choice is a function of your basic belief and core values in life. If the political crystal balls of the society beget your choice, then, you are a victim of the political system.

Africa is poor by choice, not by chance. The dominant values running to African economy, politics and social space is responsible is responsible for the following

- Thequality of people emerging into public offices

- The quality of works coming out of Africa
- The quality of news coming out from the African news media
- The quality of products and services coming out from product and service industries in Africa
- The number and quality of intellectual properties coming out of Africa
- The quality of global investments that Africa is able to attract per time
- Africa Economic rating, political rating and prevailing social realities in the regional space
- E.t.c

   It's not natural resources of a nation that actually accounts for its advancement in the affairs of life, rather is the "CRITICAL CHOICE" of the people and government that determines how well , good and peaceful the society will be. At every point in time, people and government are pouring something into the "CHOICE SPACE", and its that its cumulative choice that begets the actual realties that prevails over all in the society. The question is what is the government pouring into the nation's CHOICE SPACE?. It is creating the future of the society. It is either moving the system forward or backward. It is probably improving on the core values of the society or depreciating it. It is either empowering the citizens or disempowering them. CHOICE is the REAL WORK of leadership in the society. Africa can advance beyond the present status quo the moment the government wish the will power to disrupt the WRONG CHOICE that has created setbacks in the past.

It's possible leadership in the society sees no apparently reason to disrupt the "CHOICE SPACE" that entrenched in the system, then, …..on individual level you have to DISRUPT YOUR CHOICE. For sure you can change the society from a personal "choice space". It is the matter of clarity of vision, will power, Expertise, preservance and consistency in doing the right thing. Most advanced nations were nit changed from the top of government hierarchy, rather from individual quarters. The American market was not created practically from the WHITHOUSE in Washington D.C, rather from the American people.

In every election, the American people votes for progress, peace, better healthcare, technological expulsions, massive job creation, strong and vibrant institutions etc. in the American system the electorates are politically informed and do not go to poll with the "PARTY-THING", as obtains in Africa. Each voter in activating better future for the people of America.

The people of America in every election unanimously vote against:

- Insecurity
- Poverty
- Religious crisis
- Poor educational system
- Poor healthcare
- Poor crippled institutions
- Terrorism
- Violence

101

- Etc.

The American people understand the sensitivity of the nation "CHOICE SPACE" and individual "CHOICE SPACE" respectively I negotiating the future of the society. For the purpose of emphasis, I repeat: "it is not the natural resources of a nation that makes it emerge in the comity of advanced economy ratherIt's the cumulative choice of the people and government that negotiates the society. Therefore if the system cannot change you for good, CHANGE THE SYSTEM. You always have a choice at any time. Whenever you stop in life, it's a good personal choice. If the odds are literally against, Check yours 'CHOICE SPACE', and 'DISRUPT' it.

Any choice that prevails over you in GOVERNMENT over you. In the world of satisfaction, your choice is fundamental in negotiating for your fulfillment and happiness. Certificates do not make people but choice does. The odds in the society represent bye-products of the system CHOICE SPACE are really government itself. But you have a huge capacity to resist it and work to fulfill your destiny. That capacity is called "PERSONAL CHOICE". You can survival any blackmail in the society, but not the scandal of "POOR CHOICE" or "NO CHOICE". If the system you found yourself expose you to social embarrassment or disadvantage, you can embark on social innovative DIDRUPTION' of you "CHOICE SPACE". At all times, you can beat the "P-Suite", "(re-poor suite) facilities to create your desired world any day.

CHOICE IS FUNDEMENTAL BLOCK TO BUILD ENDURING ENTERPRISE FOR PEOPLE

In the wake 21st century super-industries economic realities, 'CHOICE-SPACE' appears to be the greatest singular and ever-green RESOURCE of any people or system. From CAIRO to CARBEANS, and AMERIC to AUSTRILIA and to the wider world, people rises into global spotlight and go down, skills, expertise and knowledge's rises and go into antiquity, but the choice bringing them up lias with them and even continue existence after they have long departed to the obligation. In the words of the Erudite Author: "Everything rises and ends with leadership".

CHOICE IS LEADERSHIP. Thus, everything rises and ends with CHOICE. TWITTER supper and is swashed with captions hash tags like:

☐ America decides
☐ South Africa decides
☐ Nigeria decides
☐ Greece decides
☐ Egypt decides, etc.

Whatever leadership team people vote into the public space is their CHOICE. Great nations and people séances their destroy by activating the POWER OF CHOICE. No matter the size or quality of natural resources located with the circumference of a nation's territory, it is CHOICE that really accounts for either setback or advancement at the end of the day. It's from the "CHOICE SPACE" the followings Emerge.

☐ Core values of the society

- Value for human lives and properties
- Value for dignity of labour
- Value for enterprise cultural operations
- Value for education
- Value for fundamental human rights
- Value for security and peace
- Value for intellectual prosperity
- Value for openness and accountability
- Value for credibility and injustice
- Value for unity and national objectives
- Etc.

On the absence of right choice, expertise is useless. If the choice is family, every other thing is faulty. If the foundation of a building is technically faulty, every other structure upon it stands upon a faulty background. That is why, when people shop around the world to get the best idea, knowledge, concept or even experts to build their society upon a faulty leadership pedigree, nothing apparently seems to work. That is also, reasons so many third world countries are where they are at the moment.

Wrong or poor leadership team can never perform wonder or magic in Africa. So long the people fit out in every election in Africa to vote for:

- Religion difference

- ☐ Ethnic difference
- ☐ Party ideology (faulty)
- ☐ Sectarin difference
- ☐ Geo-political difference
- ☐ Colour, role
- ☐ Etc.

What is striping advancement from African-Economy is the people "CHOICE SPACE"and the government "CHOICE SPACE" respectively. If evil prevails over good in the land is the function of choice enthroned in the leadership space. If mediocrity is celebrated in the open in the place of Excellence. It is the choice of the people. It is choice that builds enduring enterprise or people, not the battle for advancement were to be a game of natural resources domiciled in the territory of a nation,Nigeria sincerely lead the entice world. The country has been plagued with monstrous setback from history with "Pook choice space". There is nothing wrong with Nigerian:

- ☐ Crude oil
- ☐ Solid minerals
- ☐ Other liquid minerals
- ☐ Vegetation
- ☐ Climate
- ☐ Landmass topography
- ☐ Location
- ☐ Etc.

It has been the people "Choice space" and that of the government that is responsible for where the country is at the moment. Choice is absolutely. Africa must be prepared now and in the future to disrupt choice that clogs on the wheels of progress.

UNLEARNING YOUR MIND IS THE EASIEST WAY TO DISRUPT YOURSELF.

Whatever thing you learn gradually forms a permanent structure in your mind, and has way to influence your cultural reality. In the game of holistic innovation, mind disruption is of paramount importance than dismantling of physical realities. Learning is simple, but FOGETTING is superior. Forgetting is mentally tasking. It is simply reversing and dropping whatever realities about something that you have ingested into your mind. Forgetting is actually tougher than learning. It is a reverse protocol that must be carried out both consciously and sub-consciously.

The BIGGEST Challenge of African leadership and the people is never how to shop for new and innovative ideas to transform the region economic realities and primitive socio-political orthodoxy out of the system.

FORGETTING IS THE REAL CHALLENGE of African present reality. It is the BIG GAME the people of Africa must prepare to play of enhancement of the region must be in veins.

On a personal note, until you disrupt the ante fact of yesterday – you probably will not win the opportunities present and ahead. Your mind is the center of your life activities. To move forward in life at any time, you need to dismantle certain realities in your mind. One of those primary activities to plunge you forward in life is FORGETTING. Its error that most school systems in the third world countries have curriculum for learning, but not have curriculum to reverse learning and inspires forgetting. It's an error of a kind that keeps people in a vicious cycle.

You cannot really disrupt yourself without first disrupting the CONTENT REALITY of your mind. When you break out from the status quo you can build a new pattern to lead your freedom. You can transit from poor economy to strong and vibrant economy. Disruption of your mind is critical in enhancing your life and expanding your options for survival in life. It is a choice you have to make... to unlearn the thoughts that are sterile and unproductive in your mind. It is not seeking for a subordinate or mere alternative, rather its more of outright "BLOW OUT" of the wrong edition from your thinking, and constructive creation of innovative replacement.

" The greatest difficulty in the world is not for people to accept new ideas, but to make them forget about the old ones" John Marynard Keyness Economist

The speed with which you are able to de-construct old and expired realities from your mind, determines the speed at which you break into new and desire realities. Your ability to unlearn your mind of all the poisoned mills of the wrong school system, the background information you swallowed from your parents or other alternative figures in your early life, and the manipulations in the political scene programs you to beat the "P-CURVE" (i.e poverty curve) of the society. The poverty bug is a conscious program masterminded by someone or group to keep the rest of the society poor and miserable. In some quarters of the society, the poverty bug is a huge business. The poor people are not usually consulted while taken annual decision that affect the national economy. But, the rich and poor buy from the same market. It an intelligent development aims. You only stand a chance if you can:

☐ Disrupt you internal government …………

☐ Dismantle expired realities berthing ……… deep within you ……..

☐ De-construct your choice ………

☐ Blow out your poisoned and expired ideas ……..

☐ Break out from the unusual pattern …………

☐ Take adventure beyond mormatery …………

DISRUPT YOUR RULES:

According to Merrian Webster dictionary, rules represents:

- A statement that tells you what is or is not allowed in a particular game, situation, etc.
- A statement that tells you what is allowed or what will happen within a particular system (such) as a language or sequence.
- A prescribed ground for conduct or action.
- The laws or regulation prescribed by the founder of a religions order for observant by its members.
- An accepted procedure, custom or habit, etc.

However, for the focus of this work I want to define rules as limitations, habits, resistance and structures that acts against progress, creative innovations, enhancement, etc. At best, any rule whether circular or sacred leads you to a boundary of reality. There is a word beyond any form of boundary, and there is a codethat must be activated to attain it. This called is: "CREATIVE DISRUPTION" of rules. God created trees, ocean, the atmosphere and minerals on and beneath the earth. He only commanded the first man kind

111

Adam to trend over the garden of Eden. The word "trend" was first used in record time in 14th century, and it is intransitive verb. According to Merrian Webster dictionary, it means.

☐ To manage the operations.
☐ To prevent mischance
☐ To move, direct, or develop ones course in a particular direction
☐ To exhibit an inclination, etc.

In none material terms, to develop means to de-envelop, that is to uncover that which is hidden from the optical eyes. To subordinated the above, it means to bring out the hidden value of a thing. Therefore, the assignment God gave to mankind is to trend (i.e de-envelop, disrupt the order and to de-construct realities creatively). The Adamic word created so many things by sheer disruption of order (i.e rules) and expanded reality to the best of their knowledge or technical know-how.

RULES ARE GOVERNMENT IN ITSELF

Every society is governed by set of rules that defines "LIMITS" and "continuity". It is imperative to articulate the set of rules that inhibits your advancement from the set rules of society for instance, before now in America school dropout were never celebrated because people dropout from school in to nothing. Therefore, the system of the American default economy never favoured them. Now, in the Noake of 21st century, several folks dropped out of school, and did drop into something that eventually shifted the bound of reality on a global state. Most of the folks in the siliver valley are school dropout that turned into cooperate sell-outs. This guys have kind of constituted new government in the global market places. This is creative disruption of rules. If you cannot change the system, you stay where the system keep you. Disruption is not for everybody. Not everyone has to abandon the traditionalorder, standard and rules. If you discover that things around you are no more working as expected, or you have reached a height that you cannot see progress anymore, then you should disrupt yourself by "blowing out" the rules that kept you at the plateau of emptiness.

In the industrial age, people disrupted the trees and creatively intended tables, chairs, paper, and host of others. People disrupted the rivers and oceans, and built dams to generate electricity and constructed bridges including tunnels to reach new land mass, new market and opened up the boundaries of realities. People disrupted the earth creatively to bring about crude oil, bitumen, gold, silver, iron, steel, and others, then construction industries took off on a global scale. Creative destruction is the whole assignment of a man on earth and God gave the knowledge to make these possible. At any point in time, creative destruction brings about creative innovation and boundaries of possibilities are expanded.

TEN SIGNS THAT SHOWS YOU SHOULD DISRUPT YOURSELF (RULES).

1. Your present jobs donot improve on yourself worth, and makes you dull every day.
2. Your present job or assignment is no more challenging.

3. The people around you no longer add value to you or to your vision.

4. Your boss is becoming so "picky" about everything you do in and outside office, you did better disrupt yourself or face right sizing, left sizing, front sizing, back sizing. Any of this "signings" thing could become an intelligent excuse to sack you.

5. When you find yourself in a saturated market and your value pumanelled downwards you should disrupt yourself or the market disrupts you.

6. When in the market place, evolvingcompetition catches up with you. And all effort to above it proves fertile, you should disrupt risk being disrupted.

7. When your pay check rises without a corresponding increase in other monetary compensational factors. Life is no about salary, but access, social, and psychological

values. You should disrupt yourself.

8. When the sale peaked and refuse to go beyond certain percentage, then the disrupt the product or the market disrupt you.

9. When the promotions are no more coming as expected.

10. When you are no more happy and comfortable the things work around you.

DISRUPTIVE STRENGHT:

Not everyperson can go the long lonely path to disrupt self and tigger evaluation of innovative values to re-event self-worth. It is not a game armatures, rather for people with unrepentant passion to own responsibilities in all its dimensions and degrees. For this kind of folks, they have DISTINCTIVE STRENGHT.just like any other folk on the street, but have something edgy in their total packaging.

They have DISTINCTIVE STRENGHT just like any other folk on the street, but have something edgy in theirtotal packaging.

They have DISRUPTIVE STRENGHT. Simple! An individual's disruptice intelligence, disruptive leadership pedigree. Therefore, the major constituents of one's DISRUPTIVE STRENGHT are:

- [ ] DISRUPTIVE SKILL
- [ ] DISRUPTIVE INTELLIGENCE
- [ ] DISRUPTIVE SENSE
- [ ] STRONG DISRUPTIVE LEADERSHIP PEDIGREE

Big success or big failure after self-disruption is a function of "DISRUPTIVE STRENGHT", not "DISTINCTIVE STRENGHT". While disruptive strength is dynamic, distinctive strength is FIXED. In more material terms"DISTINCTIVE STRENGHT" represents "Fluid core" of the individual. Some people, organization and nation fears "INNOVATION" or

"CHANGE"because of the cycles of disruptions that comes with, and probably do not the capacity to handle issues.

Conversely, I will not want to go beyond the present dynamics showcase so far on this chapter, because my prime objective in this work is to create that much needed platform, critical mass information, activation energy, strategic insights and obsession to enable individual, organization and nation to CONSTRUCTIVE DISRUPTION of the present status guo.

It is time for Africa to think:

☐ CONSTRUCTIVE DISRUPTION OF OWN POLITICAL ECONOMY.

- UNLEARNING COLONIAL MENTALITY
- DE-CONSTRUCTION OF RELICIOUS POLITICAL INCLINATION
- DISRUPTION OF WITH-HUNTING POLITICS OF NO SENSE.
- DISMANTLING OF MAFIA POLITICS A.K.A "WINNING BY MEANS OF MILITANCY OR TERRORISM"
- CRIMINALIZATION OF OFFICIAL CORRUPTION
- DISRUPTION OF SECTARIAN POLITICS
- ETC.

  Note, you don't start disruption from outside, its rather an inside thing. Thus, DISRUPT YOUR

CHAPTER 7
KILL YOUR CITY GIANT

The worst case fatality of assassination happens here often on the shores and streets of Africa. It's a usual event that comes with politics, corruption and "wealth- trafficking in the region".

Well, it is not my obsession to flood you with statistics, figures, facts and graphics about the facilities of assassinations within Africa domain. The internet is already awashed with necessary data in various ambits as you might dim fit. My attraction in this chapter is to AWAKE YOUR SUB-CONCIOUSNESS to another REALM of knowledge Revelation. Therefore, my prime target is your MACHINE: "MIND". Ordinary assassin kills the "man", but the worst, deadliest and most fearful kills the man's MACHINE: "MIND".

Whoever controls the mind controls the man, and whatever that controls the mind, also controls the man. The battle of life begins and ends within the walls of the mind. The following forces have the capacity to control the mind:

- ☐ Belief system
- ☐ Faith
- ☐ Tradition
- ☐ Race
- ☐ Ethnic values
- ☐ Political government
- ☐ Ideas
- ☐ Choices
- ☐ Rules
- ☐ Habits

☐ Love
☐ Education
☐ Money, etc.

In part, some of the above listed forces have dealt with Africa, and have continued to put the continent in negative spot light. Anything that constitutes a major setback, weakness and disadvantage for a person, organization or nation is what I tagged: "CITY GIANT". What killed Ceaser were not the daggers of his assassins, but the armor of city giant. He trusted in wrong vessel, and paid with his life. His assassins conspired against him, and used the armor of city giant to bring him down. Even, Samson in the Holy Bible trapped down with love, lust his dreadlock for voice, and died for love. The worst assassin that bears the seabbard is most valuable in the presence of a city giant. Whatever that twinkles the fancy of the mind or whoever that has the capacity to twinkle the fancy of the mind inevitably "controls" and can determine the essence of realities around the man. The most gallant marksman on the street is most valuable before the city giant. The dead beast theorist is most valuable before the city giant. The most frugal leadership machine is most valuable before the city giant just every one of us is valuable. The ability to manage the degree of ones valuability before this city giant is most critical factors in every life ecology. Wherever you strapped in life is a function of your city giant. The level of your professional prowess is determined by your city giant. Your level of success or failure is the function of your city giant. Success of failure in the future is the function of the city giant. In plane words, your degree of weakness is critical in determining your actual strength and what you can survive in your life time. The speed at which each person makes on the royal high ways of destiny is determined by the relative force (s) of individuals city giant (s)."your city giant (s)"is the actual "REGULATING POWER" over your life.

DISRUPT YOUR WEAKNESS:

In a close eco-system, the best speeches that survives the turbulence time and consist moment is usually the most adaptive, and not the strongest predator. In the industrial revolution age, the greatest strategy that ruled that era is "CORE COMPETENCE", but right now at the moment in the super industrial economic revolution, the best and greatest rule of the day is. "FLUID-CORE". Anyone who has the capacity to disrupt the old and expired economic stratagem or mind set, have automatically DE-CONSTRUCT the weakness betting deep within him. That is just a giant step towards a great future. Personal weakness kills gradually, but destroys ultimately. Having a professional strength or aptitude can get you a desired job, but it is the strength of your personal weakness that can make you either a huge success or failure. Your professional problems cannot replace, overwhelm or destroy your personal weakness. It is a personal assignmentto discover your WEAKNESS and DISRUPT IT. When institutions fail to deliver on expectation, it shows off the degree of character decadence. The failure of strong institution like marriage, organization or government of nations is true reflection of failure of individual character. Every WEAKNESS is not just a thing or rather a character, And every character whether good or bad represents a kind of CITY GIANT The government of the day can feral to deliver on the mandate given to them, and that is like a dot in the life of any man, but if a man fail due to UNTAMED WEAKENESS then, everything have failed. It's difficult to manage a broken family, integrity and Excellence. Thus, it's imperative to DISRUPT your WEAKNESS before it Disrupt your future.

Any man's future is tried to his opportunities. The cumulative opportunity that anyone enjoys in lifetime is dependent not just on the strength of his technical competence, character quotient, integrity grid, but also dependent on the straight of his "PERSONAL WEAKNESS".

While it's difficult or even impossible to control or influence the decisions, policies and legislatures of the ruling powers of the day, you can always control, time and manage the WEAKNESS in your personal space. It is possible for the government to fail, but your character that gives you comparative advantage in life marketplace should not fail. It's your greatest possession. It's your most trusted ally. It's your weaponry against poverty and mediocrity.

With cleverly tamed personal weakness you can win any war on the streets of Africa. You need a personal decision to remain committed to winning the war on the shore of Africa. Tamed personal weakness positions you at huge advantage in your neighborhood, community space and in your work-space. It does not mean you are weak or causeless, rather it means that your intelligent, focus and committed to a personal WEAKNESS is the greatest victory one can win on the streets of Africa in such a critical time as this. You can take a decision not to:

- Accept bribery
- Break your marital vows
- Break oath of office
- Get involve with corruption

- Keep hoodlums as friends
- Smoke marijuana or cocaine
- Get involve in human trafficking
- Join campus or street cults
- Get involve in money cindering
- Join armed robbery gangs
- Military or any violet group
- Accept money to kill follow human being
- Workplace misconduct
- Etc.

You actually need not be a man or Revered Father to do this; of course, this is a matter of personal principle, and not some kind of church or religious thing. Living a decent life is a CHIOCE, and more of a personal decision is principled, than live in gross Indiscipline.

A failed state is a graphical representation of failed personal character, not about failed infrastructure. Any government institution that runs on power dynamics of cumulative personal weakness cannot run for a long time. Strong personal weakness is worse than the atomic bomb dropped in Hiroshima. It has the capacity to cripple an institution against all good intention cum actions. If the leadership suffers a major character deficiency, the entire system is affected by this singular WEAKNESS. For me, or government as some kind of "AIRCRAFT".

If there be a major fault unchecked, undiscovered or unfixed, everyone aboard the flight is hell bound to untimely, painful and indescribable death experiences. When any nation or institution crashes – it's actually a testament of characters failure.

It's important to disrupt your personal weakness now because of what is about of you in the future. Everything about you is rising or going down in life is tied to your ability to upset your weakness and built on your comparative advantage. If you cannot destroy your WEAKNESS, then tame it before it disrupts your future. It's your major obligation to work on your personal weakness purposefully and consciously. It's important you do not leave this to chance. A strong PERAONAL WEAKNESS is a "CITY GIANT" you must destroy first before it destroys you. Watch your back!

DECONSTRUCT YOUR DISADVANTAGES

It is important to recognize your major disadvantages in life early. Your disadvantages have the capacity to put the tides against you. It informs the very point of all attack against you in life. You must consciously mark out your very disadvantages in life, and diligently de-construct, it such that it cannot weight in anything about you. Disadvantages de-constructed are like enemies defeated. If you fail, for whatever reason to handle your disadvantages decisively on time, it will surely surprise or shock you tomorrow.

Every Nation has one, two or more disadvantages within, but good leadership would de-construct it and move the nation forward. But bad leadership can turn same into an excuse for not performing in the office. For some, it could even become a personal excuse for looting the economy dry. National transformation is all about defusing the bomb-shell called "DISADVANTAGES' personal transformation cannot happen until someone de-constructs looming disadvantages hanging around. The work of every innovator – centric leader is to really map out strategic forces around defined structures of disadvantages in any part of the society. It is the obligation of this tactician to utilize every available and reliable force to dismantle "DISAVANTAGES". A leader cannot really do much for his people in the presence of looming disadvantages hanging around. The monster will practically inhibit development and defile the guts of the mask man; except, there be a strategic master plan to disrupt it.

"DISADVANTAGES" of any kind is a development monster. For instance, poverty of good ideas, poverty of finance and ignorance has kept Africa down in terms of real big time economic and political advancement in the 21st century. Other major factors limiting the African dream development, includes:

- Corruption of office holders
- Insecurity
- Absence of peace
- Religious politics
- Tribal politics
- Sectarian politics
- Terrorism
- Destructive-self-style leadership
- Frustrated democratization process
- Inadequate international cooperation
- Inadequate technology transfer
- Poverty
- Over-population pressure
- Poor literacy level and ignorance
- Unemployment
- Hunger and food insecurity
- Destroyed traditional knowledge and spiritual heritage, etc.

The list of African disadvantages is not limited to the above listed. If African leaders have shown marked commitment in de-constructing this looming status gone from the point of self-governance, African would have lead the comity of advanced economics in the world. It appears that African leaders do not really plan well and ahead of time before emerging into government office. Also, it seems that, herd-in Africa; people do not have development agenda before emerging into the public office to serve. It is not the political party that develops the society, but the elected officers in the public offices.

Most leaders are not obsessed by anything other than self-enrichment while going into office. That is the sole reason while politics in Africa has gradually and surely degenerated into money politics. The winner takes it all. The winner is above the law and state's constituted constitutional provisions. African in global politics should this present political realities continues to thrive in the system.